W9-BBD-287

Economic Development and Environmental Protection in Latin America

Woodrow Wilson Center
Current Studies on Latin America

Published with the Latin American Program
of the Woodrow Wilson International Center for Scholars
Joseph S. Tulchin, Director

Economic Development and Environmental Protection in Latin America

edited by
Joseph S. Tulchin
with Andrew I. Rudman

Lynne Rienner Publishers ▪ Boulder & London

Published in the United States of America in 1991 by
Lynne Rienner Publishers, Inc.
1800 30th Street, Boulder, Colorado 80301

and in the United Kingdom by
Lynne Rienner Publishers, Inc.
3 Henrietta Street, Covent Garden, London WC2E 8LU

© 1991 by The Woodrow Wilson International Center for Scholars.
All rights reserved

Library of Congress Cataloging-in-Publication Data
Economic development and environmental protection in Latin America
    edited by Joseph S. Tulchin and Andrew I. Rudman
    (Woodrow Wilson Center current studies on Latin America)
    Includes bibliographical references and index.
    ISBN 1-55587-288-3
    1. Environmental policy—Economic aspects—Latin America.
2. Environmental protection—Economic aspects—Latin America.
I. Tulchin, Joseph S., 1939- . II. Rudman, Andrew I.
III. Series
HC130.E5E26   1991
363.7′056′098—dc20   91-15701
                           CIP

British Cataloguing in Publication Data
A Cataloguing in Publication record for this book
is available from the British Library.

Printed and bound in the United States of America

The paper used in this publication meets the requirements
of the American National Standard for Permanence of
Paper for Printed Library Materials Z39.48-1984.

Contents

Preface

This is the first in a series of studies on current issues published by the Latin American Program of the Woodrow Wilson Center for Scholars in conjunction with Lynne Rienner Publishers. The Latin American Program is pleased to launch this series of special studies, each of which is intended as a contribution to the public discussion of an issue of major importance. All of the studies are based on special activities of the Latin American Program, most often a conference or seminar conducted at the Woodrow Wilson Center. They are not, strictly speaking, academic works. They are, however, serious efforts to analyze issues of fundamental significance to Latin America. We hope that they will be part of a discussion in progress and of use to the policy and academic communities concerned with Latin America.

This first volume is the result of a series of seminars conducted in late 1989. Funding for the series was provided by the Inter-American Development Bank, as part of the economic issues series that the IBD sponsors. We are grateful to the IBD for its continuing support of the Woodrow Wilson Center.

Andrew I. Rudman, then program assistant of the Latin American Program, coordinated the series. Leah Florence prepared the manuscript for publication.

Joseph S. Tulchin

Introduction

—— *Joseph S. Tulchin & Andrew I. Rudman* ——

The environment has become a global issue affecting each and every one of us. Nearly every day, information about some short- or long-term threat to the environment is presented in the mass media. Concern for the environment, and how best to ward off the impending disasters of which the scientific community warns us, has become an integral part of public debate among academic specialists and the policymaking community. The growing public concern with the greenhouse effect and the deforestation of the Amazon, two of the most publicized environmental issues, has forced academics and policymakers to focus greater attention and resources on the environment. Advanced scientific research, policy studies, and numerous conferences and seminars designed to promote environmental awareness have been conducted around the world. These issues are indeed global, crossing national and international boundaries with no respect for strategic alliances or political ideology. The environment affects us all, and thus a cross-disciplinary and cross-regional approach is essential if we are to achieve the degree of understanding necessary to formulate effective environmental public policies.

In Latin America, fear is widespread that efforts to protect the environment somehow will impede or frustrate plans for economic development. For many years, environmental concerns were the monopoly of small, single-issue, often economically privileged groups in the industrialized nations—the "Greens" in Europe, for example, and wildlife groups in the United States. Third World nations considered such concerns a luxury. Indeed, in international forums, representatives of developing nations in Latin America often referred to concern for the environment as yet another means by which the industrialized North would keep the underdeveloped South in thrall.

Recently, this situation has begun to change. Latin Americans have begun to address environmental issues previously ignored or considered

Joseph S. Tulchin is director of the Latin American Program of the Woodrow Wilson Center; Andrew I. Rudman, previously program associate of the Woodrow Wilson Center Latin American Program, is now with the US Foreign Service posted to Guayaquil, Ecuador.

1

in conflict with their desperate need for economic growth. The worldwide concern about the depletion of the ozone layer has led to greater attention to and emphasis on the deforestation of the Amazon basin in Latin American as well as industrialized nations. These environmental issues have stirred a number of controversies in the region. Many Latin Americans believe that the industrialized nations have no right to urge them to impose restrictions on the use of their land while the imperial powers continue to exploit their own land as they have done since colonial times. The need for Latin America, and all of the developing world, to find new sources of economic growth is also raised in the context of environmental protection. Most central to the debate and most controversial is the question of how the concern for the environment can be reconciled with the need of some nations to exploit their own national resources to achieve the growth necessary to improve the lives of their citizens.

The threat to the environment created by economic development programs has just begun to receive international attention and concern. Air emissions standards and controls are an extremely sensitive issue, especially along international borders such as between the United States and Mexico or among the nations of Europe. Controlling the flow of water on the branches of the River Plata estuary has been at issue among Brazil, Paraguay, Uruguay, and Argentina for two decades. The rapid shift from subsistence farming to commercial export-oriented agriculture has contributed to a massive exodus from the land to already overcrowded urban centers such as Mexico City. An accelerating soil depletion has exacerbated tensions among Central American nations as well as between them and Mexico on the one hand, and the United States on the other. The debt crisis has been viewed by some as an opportunity to force Latin American (and possibly Eastern European) nations to adopt new environmental protection laws in return for debt relief or renegotiation through debt-for-nature swaps. These debt-for-nature swaps have been used extensively in Ecuador, Costa Rica, and Bolivia. They underline both the interrelationship between economic development and environmental protection and the international nature of environmental issues.

Latin America exhibits special characteristics in regard to the potential threat to economic development that is posed by environmental protection. The increased attention paid to Brazil's environmental policy is but one example of this significance. By the year 2000, eighteen of the world's twenty-one largest cities will be in the Southern Hemisphere. Two of these, Mexico City and São Paulo, are already being forced to respond to the environmental crisis as it applies to air and water quality, sanitation, and land use. Although these cities may be the ones most in need of solutions, the problems they face are shared to some degree by all of the region's major cities. The urgent need to respond to the urban crisis after a decade of economic stagnation has led to innovative solutions, often at the local level, to the environmental problems affecting the region's cities. Thus Latin America can serve as a laboratory model for the developing or the developed worlds.

The Latin American Program of the Woodrow Wilson Center seeks to promote enhanced discussion and sharpened analysis of public policy in order to assist policymakers in reaching the decisions necessary to reconcile economic growth and environmental protection. To that end, a series of four roundtable discussions on a range of environmental topics with a Latin American focus was held in the fall of 1989. The roundtables, called the Economic Development and Environmental Protection Series, formed part of the Economic Issues Series and were cosponsored by the World Bank and the Inter-American Development Bank. The sessions focused on (1) a theoretical and practical discussion of sustainable development practices, (2) deforestation and alternative land use, (3) debt-for-nature swaps in Latin America and Eastern Europe, and (4) air pollution control measures in Mexico City and Los Angeles.

Session one was devoted to sustainable development practices. The speakers included Sen. Timothy Wirth (D-Colo.), Dr. Herman Daly of the World Bank, and Dr. Thomas Tietenberg of Colby College. Dr. Jessica Mathews of the World Resources Institute acted as commentator for the session.

Sen. Wirth stressed that the United States must clean up its "own backyard" and act as an example to the developing world. He also quoted Brazilian President José Sarney, who asked that the Amazon not become a "green Persian Gulf," and emphasized that we also must be sensitive to the needs and opinions of other governments. This is perhaps the single most important theme in the series.

Dr. Daly emphasized the need to define sustainable development. He also urged policymakers to recognize the distinction between growth, which is finite, and development, which means, as defined by the Brundtland Commission, "development that meets the needs of the present without compromising the ability of the future to meet its own needs."

Dr. Tietenberg discussed economic incentives policies and their potential for helping to improve environmental conditions in an economically efficient manner. Convincing policymakers that environmental protection can be economically efficient, the second important theme of the first session, is repeated throughout the series. Policies regarding transportation, emissions, and technology in the United States must be reevaluated in order to put our house in order from an

3

environmental standpoint.

The deforestation of the Amazon was the topic of session two. The speakers included Dr. Kari Keipi of the Inter-American Development Bank, Dr. John Browder of Virginia Polytechnic Institute, and Mr. Tadeu Valadares of the Brazilian embassy in Washington, D.C. Commentary was provided by Dr. Marc Dourojeanni of the World Bank.

Dr. Keipi defined the causes of deforestation as population pressure, poverty, unsecured land tenure, lack of technological and environmental awareness, lack of financing for small farmers, and misguided agricultural policies. Dr. Browder suggested that deforestation is the product of troubling economic, social, and political issues including rural poverty, rapid population growth, food and energy deficiency, territorial sovereignty, debt, and modernization policies. Mr. Valadares placed population pressure and cattle ranching, together with inadequate resources to enforce existing laws, above all other explanations for deforestation. A review of the panelists' opinions suggests that agreement on the causes of deforestation may be an important prerequisite to solving the problem.

Dr. Keipi identified the policy options to prevent or reduce deforestation that are endorsed by the Inter-American Development Bank. These include improved forest management, alternate energy sources, and the protection of tropical forests from highway projects. Mr. Valadares identified Brazil's efforts to define the areas to be protected and to pursue and prosecute those engaged in illegal burning activities. The Brazilian government is also trying to relieve land pressure on the Amazon by accelerating land reform in other parts of Brazil better suited to agricultural production. Dr. Browder offered a different perspective, suggesting that the entire concept of development must be redefined to reflect policies that will benefit the indigenous peoples of the rainforest and de-emphasize traditional measurements of growth.

Despite holding different opinions on the causes of and solutions to deforestation, the panelists agreed on some specific factors necessary to halt the spread of deforestation. These measures include increased indigenous involvement in the forest management process, effective land control, cash-crop production, and new development policies that can relieve the demand on the forests for immediate economic gratification.

Session three was devoted to a discussion of the pros and cons of debt-for-nature swaps. Speakers included Congressman John Porter (R-Ill.), Dr. Richard Liroff of the Conservation Foundation/World Wildlife Fund, and Dr. Bruce Rich of the Environmental Defense Fund. The commentator was the originator of the debt-for-nature concept, Dr. Thomas Lovejoy of the Smithsonian Institution. The session focused on how the swaps have been used in the past to protect environmentally sensitive areas and how their use can be expanded.

Dr. Lovejoy stressed that the ultimate goal of the swaps is financial and they should not be construed as an "environmental Louisiana Purchase," which would create vast tracts of protected land. Congressman Porter agreed that debt-for-nature does not mean debt-for-do-not-touch. He stressed that the land is to be protected and used for the benefit of the country and its inhabitants in a sustainable manner, and the involvement of indigenous groups is essential to the success of a debt-swap project.

Dr. Liroff presented a review of the debt-for-nature swap possibilities for Poland, pointing out some of the differences between Eastern European and Latin American debt swaps, but stressing that the intent—sustainable use—is identical. He echoed the views of speakers from previous sessions who urged multinational cooperation and the involvement of indigenous groups in the decisionmaking process.

Dr. Rich analyzed US economic policy in connection with debt swaps and environmental protection. He acknowledged that the swaps make only a small dent in the debt burden faced by Latin America but suggested that the Brady Plan may allow for greater debt swap reliance through its debt repurchase component. He stressed that debt-for-nature swaps are not a solution to the debt crisis, but they can play an important role in achieving sustainable development. He stated that cooperation with debtor country governments is necessary for the swaps to be an effective means of promoting economic growth and environmental protection.

The final session was devoted to the issue of air pollution, especially in Mexico City where the problem, although not unique, is most acute. The speakers included Lic. Fernando Menéndez Garza of the government of Mexico City, Dr. Richard Nuccio of Georgetown University, and Mr. Robert Yuhnke of the Environmental Defense Fund. Commentary was provided by Dr. Rene Costales of the Inter-American Development Bank.

Lic. Menéndez summarized Mexico City's efforts to combat its severe air pollution problems, which are caused by a variety of factors including population growth, the city's geographic characteristics, and erosion. Mexico City already has implemented a number of programs designed to reduce air pollution including the use of improved fuels, the promotion of natural gas over oil, renovation of the urban bus fleet, and parking prohibitions in certain downtown areas. Perhaps most interesting is a program that removes all vehicles from city streets one day per week in December, January, and February, the months in which air quality is most precarious.

Dr. Nuccio argued that other causes of the air pollution problems are related more closely to the economic policies followed by the Mexican government. He specifically cited the import-substitution industrialization policies of the 1960s, which favored industrialization and urban development over agriculture and rural development, resulting in intense migration into Mexico City. The poles of economic growth simultaneously became the poles of environmental damage.

Mr. Yuhnke discussed the air pollution problems that face Los Angeles, noting that because Los Angeles and Mexico City are of similar scale, comparisons between the two are valid. He presented an impassioned plea for the redefinition of US transportation policy, which is too heavily geared toward passenger vehicles. Like Dr. Tietenberg in session one, Yuhnke argued that environmentally sound technology can be economically cost effective. The need to reorient our policies and assume global leadership for environmental protection, stressed by Nuccio and Yuhnke, is a theme that recurs throughout the series.

Each section of this book is devoted to one of the four sessions of the series and includes edited versions of the papers presented and the remarks made by the commentators. Summaries of the discussion periods at the conclusion of each session, written by Latin American Program Associate Andrew Rudman, follow each section.

Publication of this book allows the Latin American Program of the Woodrow Wilson Center to make a contribution to the protection of the environment. By linking experts and policymakers, the project will make a lasting impact on US policy regarding sustainable development for Latin America. This publication also presents new insights into the numerous problems that face Latin America as we enter the 1990s.

PART 1

BALANCING ECONOMIC DEVELOPMENT AND ENVIRONMENTAL PROTECTION

1

A Legislative Perspective

Timothy E. Wirth

Environmental issues emerged rapidly in the 1980s and will be at the forefront of what will be going on in the 1990s in the United States, in Europe, and, hopefully, in Japan. What happens in the developing world will depend largely on how the developed world handles those issues and links its environmental concerns with the economic concerns, particularly the debt concerns, in the developing world.

I was recently in Meeker, a small community in western Colorado that had not been visited by a United States senator since the mid-1960s. I expected a discussion of cattle issues—European import quotas, or the fact that the Japanese were not buying as much Colorado beef as they should. This was not the case. The sixty people who attended the meeting in the back of the local post office wanted to talk about global warming, the impact it would have on their ability to grow crops, and the effect it would have on their water. I was delighted that these issues were being discussed in rural Colorado. It tells us that environmental issues are among the deep concerns of that electorate. As an electorate crosses the threshold of being concerned about the environment to doing something about it, the issue becomes how to mobilize forces so that people can in fact do something. Popular action must coincide with the orchestration of public policy to be truly effective in changing the nature of our institutions so that they begin to deal adequately with environmental issues.

In the United States we have focused on environmental issues predominantly from the perspective of a central headquarters command control. The theory has been that the Environmental Protection Agency (EPA) or some other government agency would define various issues and solutions, the states would act accordingly, and the world would be a better place as a consequence. Now, however, we have moved beyond that approach, and it is imperative that we look at how we can harness

Timothy E. Wirth is a member of the US Senate from Colorado.

the private sector and decentralize the decisionmaking process more effectively than we have before. It is my belief—and this is shared by an increasing number of people on Capitol Hill—that we cannot solve these environmental problems unless we enlist the forces of the marketplace. We have unleashed marketplace forces in just about every other sector of the economy—why not do this for the environment as well?

In 1988, Senator John Heinz (R-Pa.) and I put together a study called "Project 88," which examined sixteen environmental issues. The study tried to identify where we might decentralize decisionmaking, get rid of government subsidies, and allow market forces to help solve the problems under consideration. President Bush picked up part of this in the Clean Air Act. His proposal on acid rain contained a section on tradable permits, which effectively said that the government will set the goal for how much sulfur dioxide will be taken out of the air (a reduction from twenty-two million tons to twelve million tons was proposed), but it will be left to the marketplace to determine how it will be distributed across the utilities that are affected. This approach, according to various economic estimates, would save $1.5–3.5 billion a year simply through the use of tradable permits instead of a traditional command and control approach.

We would like to move forward from this juncture. In considering recycling and incentives to continue the process, we should consider removing the federal subsidies that exist in various places for doing things that in fact are damaging to the environment. This occurs in my area of the West in particular. The most egregious example is much of the timbering done across the country. This is counterproductive in terms of protecting the environment and the wrong way to spend taxpayers' money. When we start looking at these issues through an economic lens, the values are going to change.

The policy proposals we have endorsed will require a very different mind set. It is difficult to persuade people in the United States that short-term economic gain should not drive all public policy decisions, and particularly difficult in the West because we have habitually provided massive subsidies to pay for the extraction of resources. Thus we must develop a political environment in the United States that is conducive to long-term thinking. If that is difficult for the United States, I can understand how difficult it is for the developing world to create the necessary political environment.

In January 1989, I led a group of senators to Brazil to study the issue of debt-for-nature swaps and to try to understand what was happening in the Amazon. Our guide was Thomas Lovejoy, the "father" of debt-for-nature swaps. We had a long discussion with President José Sarney in which he made two important points about the Amazon. First, he said that the Amazon should not become a "green Persian Gulf"—a legitimate reflection of Brazil's sense of nationalism about the Amazon. Second, he asked us why we came to tell him what to do with the Brazilian rainforest when we were tearing down the last great rainforest in North America, the Tongass National Forest in southern Alaska. He was absolutely correct.

We are doing exactly what we are telling the Brazilians not to do. We must better manage the resources in the North American rainforest, as well as work with the Brazilians to help them do the same in the Amazon. Rather than tearing down the Tongass National Forest for its very short-term timber value, we should manage its resources. For example, the Tongass surrounds the streams to which the salmon come back every three years to spawn. Removing trees imperils the streambed, thereby affecting an enormous and productive fish industry. If we destroy the forest in southern Alaska, we will destroy the habitat for big game and thus jeopardize the environment, tourism, and recreation. Rather than extracting the products of the rainforests, we should prospect them for the biological diversity found there.

We must also address the population issue. One should, perhaps, start with the central thesis that the world's population must be controlled. Unfortunately, we are not going to be able to make any progress on that front until the current administration decides to move away from its current policy. Without leadership from the White House, it will be impossible for us to do much more than make some very superficial changes around the edges.

We have a lot of work to do in our own backyard to be an example to the rest of the world if we believe that we should continue to lead. To do so demands a change of attitude in Congress and greater leadership emanating from the White House. Our responsibility in the United States is to set a reasonable example for the rest of the world and to help develop the instruments to provide financial flexibility so that the world's natural resources can be used to provide long-term, environmentally benign returns.

2

The Role of the Multilateral Lending Agency

Herman Daly

The World Bank has come under a great deal of criticism for its past environmental activities and even some of its present activities. It is important to keep us honest. I would like to suggest that the problem we are facing with balancing economic development and environmental protection is rooted in the university departments of economics where most of the people at the Bank were educated.

The fundamental starting point of economic analysis, if you look at any textbook, is a circular flow diagram. Circular flow of exchange value goes from firms to households and from households to firms, with no inlets or outlets, nothing coming in from the outside and nothing going to the outside. It has no possibility of ever interacting with the environment. We must move away from that basic vision and consider the economy not as an isolated system, but rather as an open subsystem of the total ecosystem that lives off the total system through an exchange of materials and energy. Until we take that interpretation as our preanalytic vision, we are going to have a difficult time dealing with environmental problems. They will always be brought in as afterthoughts and externalities treated on an ad hoc basis.

I recently gave a presentation in Canada on the question of sustainable development—the attempt to resolve the conflict between economic development and environmental protection. Afterward, a member of the audience told me: "What really worries me is that you are trying to pursue the idea of sustainable development in the Third World. But where it ought to be pushed first is in the industrialized world, and you are in no position to do that." That was challenging indeed. The World Bank can put environmental conditions on loans to the Third World, but what can it do with respect to the industrialized countries? We run into the problem that President Sarney presented to Senator Wirth—we expect the Third World to adopt constraints on their

Herman Daly is senior economist with the Environmental Department of the World Bank.

economic activity that we did not have and do not have even now.

The Brundtland Commission defined sustainable development as "development that meets the needs of the present without compromising the ability of the future to meet its own needs." Although this definition cannot be improved upon, it is important to consider that sustainability represents equity with respect to the future—dealing the future into the distributional equation. It is important to emphasize this because very often sustainability is seen as a diversion of attention away from issues of equity toward some other issues.

Because sustainable development is now the official policy of the World Bank and the United Nations, it is a practical necessity to define that concept clearly and operationally. The following short definition, as a preliminary suggestion, contains a few terms that require their own definition. First, "to develop" means to expand or realize the potentialities of, and to bring gradually to a fuller, greater, or better state. This must be contrasted with the word "grow," which means to increase in size by the addition of material through assimilation or accretion. As Kenneth Boulding says, when something grows it gets bigger. The size increase has physical material dimensions, whereas development is a qualitative improvement. "To sustain" means to keep in existence, to maintain, and to prolong. One last word that requires definition is "scale"—a short-hand term for the human presence in the biosphere, which is measured by population multiplied by per capita resource use. And resource use is the total volume of materials and energy that flow from the ecosystem through the human economy and then back to the ecosystem again as waste. A given scale could thus consist of either many people consuming at low per capita levels or fewer people consuming at high per capita levels.

Based on the preceding definitions, sustainable development is a process in which qualitative development is maintained and prolonged while quantitative growth in the scale of the economy becomes increasingly constrained by the capacity of the ecosystem to perform essential functions over the long run—that is, to regenerate the raw material input and to absorb waste outputs of the human economy. This definition invokes the distinction between growth and development. The planet Earth develops, it changes qualitatively, it evolves but it does not grow—the mass, the material, stays the same. A rolling snowball or a cancer grows but does not develop, it gains size simply by accretion. A child grows and develops at the same time.

By this definition, sustainable growth is a contradiction in terms. Growth cannot be sustained over a long period whereas development can be sustained. In fact, it is precisely the nonsustainability of physical growth that gives urgency to the concept of sustainable development.

Earth will not tolerate the doubling of even one grain of wheat sixty-four times. Yet in the past two centuries we have developed a culture that is dependent upon exponential growth. So sustainable development is a cultural adaptation made by society as it becomes aware of the emerging necessity of nongrowth in this physical sense.

Because growth so often is associated with "most," it is usually thought of in terms of gross national product (GNP). Growth in the sustainable development context does not mean growth in GNP. GNP is a mixture of physical change and nonphysical (qualitative) change, and because physical and nonphysical change are subject to very different laws and constraints, it is important to separate them, as is done in this distinction between growth and development. The distinction becomes totally blurred if you try to make development or growth refer solely to GNP because GNP mixes these two elements. So growth in this sense is not sustainable, but development can be. Indeed, even green growth is not really sustainable. There is a limit to the population of trees that Earth can support, just as there is a limit to the population of humans or automobiles that it can support.

An economy in sustainable development adapts and improves in knowledge, organization, technical efficiency, and wisdom. It does this without assimilating or accreting into itself an ever greater percentage of the matter energy of the ecosystem. Rather it stops at a scale relative to the rest of the ecosystem at which that remaining ecosystem—the environment—can continue to function and to renew itself year after year.

This raises the question of an economy growing to some kind of scale limit. We do not really know how to define an optimal scale because economic theory focuses almost entirely on optimal allocation. (It also talks about distribution, which is a separate issue.) It really does not talk about optimal scale at all, except the scale of a firm or a plant. The total economy, the aggregate macroeconomy, is really not thought of in terms of reaching some optimal scale but simply as something that continues to grow.

Two definitions of an optimal scale, neither of which is well articulated, deserve consideration. One might be called anthropocentric. The rule here would be to expand the scale of the human economy—that is to grow—to the point at which the marginal benefit to human beings of additional man-made physical capital is just equal to the marginal cost to human beings of sacrificing natural capital. So, all nonhuman species and their habitats would be valued only instrumentally according to their capacity to satisfy or to serve human wants. Their intrinsic value, their capacity to enjoy their own lives, is assumed to be zero. The other concept might be called biocentric. Under this scale, other species and their habitats would be preserved beyond the point necessary just to avoid ecological collapse and beyond the point of maximum instrumental convenience to human beings. This would stem from a recognition, however vague, that other species have intrinsic value independent of their instrumental value to human beings. Within the biocentric option, the scale of the human niche would be smaller than within the anthropocentric optimum. The definition of sustainable development given here does not specify which notion of optimum should be selected. There are further difficulties in making this definition operational. The rule for exploitation of renewable resources should be one of sustainable yield. One of the ways to control the exploitation of nonrenewable resources is to exploit them in a quasi-sustainable manner by limiting the rate of depletion to the rate at which renewable substitutes can be created. This rule needs to be defined more fully. The only thing we know for certain is that whichever scale and resource exploitation rule we choose ought to be sustainable; that, for now, is a difficult proposition.

Note

Herman Daly's comments in this chapter are his own and do not necessarily reflect the views of the World Bank.

3

The Role of Economic Incentives Policy

Thomas H. Tietenberg

Environmental regulators and lobbying groups with special interests in environmental protection in the United States traditionally have looked upon the market system as a powerful and potentially dangerous adversary. That the market unleashed powerful forces was widely recognized, and that those forces clearly acted to degrade the environment was widely lamented. Meanwhile, growth proponents have traditionally seen environmental concerns as blocking projects that had the potential to raise living standards significantly. Conflict and confrontation became the modus operandi for dealing with this clash of objectives.

The climate for dealing effectively with these concerns has improved dramatically within the last few years. Not only have growth proponents learned that in many cases short-term wealth enhancement projects that degrade the environment are ultimately counterproductive, but environmental groups have come to realize that poverty itself is a major threat to environmental protection. No longer is the issue of economic development and environmental protection seen as an "either-or" proposition. Sustainability has become an important, if still somewhat vaguely defined, criterion for choosing among alternative growth paths.[1] Rather, the focus has shifted toward the identification of policies or policy instruments that can promote the alleviation of poverty and at the same time protect the environment.

One approach that is generating a great deal of interest is known generically as an economic incentives approach to environmental regulation. Instead of mandating prescribed actions, such as requiring the installation of a particular piece of control equipment, which is the more traditional form of regulation, environmental objectives are achieved by changing the economic incentives of the agents. This can be done with fees or charges, transferable permits, or even liability law. By changing the incentives agents face, they can use their typically superior informa-

Thomas H. Tietenberg is professor of economics at Colby College.

tion to select the best means of meeting their assigned responsibilities.

Environmental groups and regulators have come to realize that the power of the market can be harnessed to achieve environmental goals, not by blocking economic growth but by channeling economic growth into more environmentally benign paths. This change in attitude has been triggered by a recognition that a former adversary, the market, can be turned into a powerful ally. Among their other virtues, approaches relying on economic incentives can reduce the conflict between environmental protection and economic development, can ease the transition to a sustainable (rather than exploitive) relationship between the economy and the environment, and can encourage the development of new, more environmentally benign production processes. Economic incentives approaches have been used in the United States and Europe since the mid-1970s, giving us a wealth of experience with how they work in practice.[2]

To be sure, experiences in one country do not automatically transfer to another. The translation of experiences from heavily industrialized nations to less industrialized nations is particularly difficult. Differences in cultural traditions, stages of development, and political superstructure, to name but a few, are formidable barriers to the diffusion of ideas. But we have discovered that at least a portion of what we have learned is relevant.

If scientists are correct in their assessment of the impact of human activities on the greenhouse effect, the industrialized world has engaged in a development path that in some ways ill prepares it for the future. As the necessity for limiting carbon dioxide intensifies, the types of high-energy, fossil fuel–based production processes that are currently the rule will experience a relative decline in competitiveness as their true social costs become recognized and internalized. Transforming an existing industrial structure and repositioning it for the future will be an expensive proposition. The less industrialized nations have an advantage in that they can design their industrial base to deal with the environmental realities of the future. Anticipating change is almost always cheaper than retrofitting. For instance, recycling was not common in the past, so manufacturers paid no attention to whether their products could be easily recycled. The market pressures they faced placed no value on recyclability. This has changed as disposal costs have begun to rise. Recyclability is becoming a valued characteristic, and those companies that anticipated this development are gaining a competitive edge.

I recently had the opportunity to consult for Sweden and for the state of California on ways to bring air quality under control. The contrast between the problems these two governments faced was striking. Sweden has high gasoline prices and a well-developed public transit system.

Swedish land-use patterns are configured to take advantage of this system. Los Angeles, on the other hand, is a city that depends almost exclusively on the automobile—it is so spread out and the population is so dispersed that a public transit alternative is difficult to implement. Efficient use of mass transit requires high-density travel corridors, a condition that exists in much of Sweden but not in Los Angeles. The regulators in Los Angeles face a much more difficult problem, not only because of the rather unique geography of their city (the aspect of most press attention) but also because existing land-use patterns reduce the possible control options significantly. The dispersed development, which was made possible by low gasoline prices, has made achieving the ambient standards much more difficult and much more expensive than had the same population been encompassed within a more energy-efficient land-use pattern from the beginning.

How can economic incentives be used to provide the signals that will make sustainable development possible? Perhaps the best way to answer this question is to share a few examples of how this approach has worked in practice. One application involves the use of an economic incentives approach to reduce the stress on an already overexploited renewable resource. The Pacific salmon, a particularly desirable fish species, can be found in the waters off the Pacific Northwest region of the United States. Due to its desirability and the traditional open access to the fishery, the salmon population was being seriously overfished. The need to reduce the pressure being put on the salmon population was rather obvious, but the means to accomplish that reduction was not. Although it was relatively easy to prevent new fishermen from entering fisheries, it was more difficult to figure out how to reduce the number of those who had been fishing in the area for years or even decades. Because fishing is characterized by economies of scale, reducing everyone's catch proportionately would simply place higher costs on everyone and waste fishing capacity as all boats sat idle for a significant proportion of time. A better solution would be to have fewer boats harvesting the stock. That way each boat could be used closer to its full capacity without depleting the salmon population. But which fisherman should be asked to give up their livelihood and leave the industry?

The economic incentives approach addressed this problem by imposing a small tax on all Pacific salmon harvested from the fishery. The revenues derived from this tax were used to buy out fishermen who were willing to forgo any future Pacific salmon fishing. Essentially fishermen stated the lowest price that they would accept for leaving the industry; the regulators selected those who could be induced to leave at the lowest price, paid the stipulated amount from the tax revenues, and retired their licenses. It was not long before a sufficient number of licenses had been retired and the salmon population was protected. Because the program was voluntary, those who left the industry did so only when they felt they had been adequately compensated. Meanwhile, those who paid the tax realized that this small investment would benefit them greatly in the future as the fish population recovered. A difficult and potentially dangerous pressure on a valuable natural resource had been avoided by the creative use of an approach that changed the economic incentives.

Economic incentives can be used not only to reduce the conflict between economic development and environmental protection, but also to make economic development the vehicle by which greater environmental protection is achieved. In the mid-1970s, several geographic regions in the United States found themselves in violation of the ambient air quality standards that had been designed to protect human health. At that point the law provided that new industries would not be allowed to move into these areas if they added any more of the pollutant responsible for the standard being violated. Because even those potential entrants adopting the most stringent control technologies would typically add some of the pollutant, this was a serious political blow to mayors eager to expand their employment and tax base. How could they allow economic growth while assuring that air quality would steadily improve to the level dictated by the ambient standard?

To respond, regulators adopted the economic incentives approach known as the "offset policy." Under this policy, firms already established in the polluted areas that voluntarily chose to control their emissions more than required under the prevailing regulations would be allowed to have the excess emission reduction certified as "emission reduction credits." Once certified, the operating permits of these firms would be tightened to assure that the reductions were permanent. The emission reduction credits could then be sold to new firms seeking to move in; they would have to buy 1.2 emission reduction credits for each 1.0 units of emissions they would add. Air quality thus improved every time a new firm moved into the area.

Although definitive data are not available, several estimates suggest that some two thousand or more offset transactions have taken place. With this policy the confrontation between economic growth and environmental protection was defused. New firms not only were allowed to move into polluted cities, they became one of the main vehicles for improving the quality of the air. Economic growth facilitated, rather than blocked, air quality improvement.

Not long after this episode, it became clear that much tighter controls would have to be placed on older, established sources of pollution in those areas still in violation of the standards. However, it would be difficult for regulators to allocate additional controls among the sources because the number of emitters was extremely diverse, the menu of technologies was vast, and regulatory staffs were too small to pick out the best technology in each setting.

The solution was to put the market to work under what is now known as the bubble policy. First, emission standards were imposed on the established sources in the most reasonable manner possible, recognizing that in practice many of these standards would inevitably turn out to be unreasonable in the glare of hindsight. Established sources were then encouraged to create "emission reduction credits" for emission reductions over and above those required by the standards. Once certified, these credits could be stored for subsequent use by the creating source when it wished to expand or could be transferred to another source for its use in meeting its standard. Because sources that could control their emissions relatively cheaply generally created and sold these credits, and sources that found themselves confronting very expensive options bought the credits in lieu of installing unreasonably expensive equipment, the costs of meeting the ambient standards were considerably lower than they would have been if the standards had been imposed and no transfers had been permitted. As a side benefit, fewer firms sought to contest their standards because this policy made it cheaper to comply than to litigate. Air quality was protected while compliance costs were reduced.

This policy has also introduced some extremely beneficial flexibility into the regulatory process. One of the emission reduction credit trades, for example, involved a firm that planned to shut down operations at one plant and build a new one. Under the old regulations, that firm either would be required to install very expensive pollution control equipment at its old plant—equipment that would be absolutely useless once the new plant was built—or it would simply be let off the hook until the new plant was built, possibly encouraging some foot-dragging in the construction process. With the bubble policy the plant was allowed to lease emission reduction credits from another nearby facility. By acquiring these credits the source guaranteed that the region benefited from the cleaner air that it would have received if it had been forced to install the temporary equipment, but at much lower cost and waste of resources. Additionally, because financial outlays were required to acquire these credits for the entire time until the new plant was operating, no incentive for foot-dragging was created.

Another source of flexibility introduced by this approach involves the capacity to control previously unregulated sources. This may be a particularly appealing attribute for those countries with currently under-developed environmental regulatory systems. For a number of reasons, ranging from the financial difficulties faced by a firm to a failure by regulators to recognize a particular pollution source, some sources are either not regulated or are regulated less than would be socially desirable. The Emissions Trading Program, the umbrella program that contains both the bubble and offset policies described above, provided a solution. Immune sources could voluntarily control their emissions more than required by their standards and sell the credits to other sources, who would gladly purchase the credits because this was significantly cheaper than controlling their own emissions to a higher degree. In this way those firms that were already subject to a high degree of control avoided having to ratchet their own controls up ever further to unreasonable levels to compensate for the lack of control in immune firms. In essence, the responsibility for identifying additional sources of control had been transferred to the market.

The characteristic of emissions trading that makes this flexibility possible is its ability to separate the question of what control is undertaken from the question of who ultimately pays for it. This is potentially important, not only in terms of domestic environmental policy but also in terms of international environmental policy. Suppose, for example, that an international agreement is ultimately signed requiring some reduction in the expected growth of carbon dioxide emissions. One proposal for achieving these reductions envisions creating a version of the offset policy for use in holding the emissions of greenhouse gases at their current levels. Under this proposal, major new sources of greenhouse gases would be required to offset their emissions, assuring that the total emissions would not increase. Offsets could be generated by conservation, by recycling, or by retiring older, heavily emitting plants. In the case of carbon dioxide, major new emitters could even invest in tree plantations, which would tend to absorb the excess gas.[3]

By creating a new market for these offsets, an incentive to invest in offset-creating activities would be stimulated.[4] Meanwhile the higher prices associated with creating the greenhouse gases, due to the need to acquire offsets, would stimulate the creators to search for ways to reduce their emissions. Transferable offsets would therefore simultaneously encourage both source control and mitigating strategies.

Because the greenhouse gas pollutants are global in nature (the location of the emissions does not matter), global markets in offsets would be possible. This is a tremendously powerful characteristic because larger markets offer the opportunity for larger cost savings. Furthermore, by selling offsets Third World countries could undertake environmentally sound investments (such as reforestation or protecting forests scheduled for harvest) that were financially underwritten by the developed world.

Another rather different example of how this concept can be applied involves water conservation in arid regions. In some parts of the United States well-intentioned regulations had an unintentional side effect—they discouraged water conservation even when water was scarce. On January 17, 1989, a historic agreement was negotiated between a growers association—a major user of irrigation water—and the Metropolitan Water District (MWD) of California—a public agency that supplies water to the Los Angeles area. Under that agreement, the MWD bears the capital and operating costs, as well as the indirect costs (such as reduced hydropower), of a huge program to reduce seepage losses as the water is transported to the growers and to install new water conserving irrigation techniques. In return they get all of the conserved water. Everyone gains. The district gets the water it needs at a reasonable price, and the growers get virtually the same amount of irrigation benefits as they got before without being forced to bear large additional expenditures that would be difficult to pass along to consumers.

The courts are beginning to get into the act as well; judicial remedies for environmental problems are beginning to take their place alongside regulatory remedies. Take, for example, the problem of cleaning up toxic waste sites that have already been closed. Current US law allows the government to sue all potentially responsible parties who contributed to the contaminated site (such as waste generators or disposal site operators). These suits accomplish a double purpose: (1) they assure that the financial responsibility for contaminated sites is borne by those who directly caused the problem; and (2) they encourage those who are currently using those sites to exercise great care, lest they be forced to bear a large financial burden in the event of an incident. The traditional remedy of going to the taxpayers would have resulted in less revenue raised, fewer sites restored, and less adequate incentives for users to exercise care.

Europe has tended to depend more on another type of economic incentive—the effluent or emission charge. This approach places a fee on each unit of pollution discharged. Faced with the responsibility for paying for the damage caused by their pollution, firms recognize the fee as a normal cost of doing business. This recognition triggers a search for possible ways to reduce the damage, including changing inputs, changing the production process, transforming the residuals to less harmful substances, and recycling by-products. The experience in the Netherlands, a country where the fees are higher than in most other countries, suggests that the effects can be dramatic.

These fees have another desirable attribute—they raise revenue. Successful development, particularly sustainable development, requires a symbiotic partnership between the public and private sectors. To function as an equal partner, the public sector must be adequately funded. If it fails to raise adequate revenue, the public sector becomes a drag on the growth process; if it raises revenue in ways that distort incentives, that too can act as a drag on development. Effluent or emission charges offer the realistic opportunity to raise revenue for the public sector without producing inefficient incentives. Whereas other types of taxation discourage growth by penalizing legitimate development incentives, emission or effluent charges provide incentives for sustainable development. Some work from the United States suggests that the drag on development avoided by substituting effluent or emission charges for more traditional revenue-raising devices, such as capital gains, income, and sales taxes, could be significant.

Incentives for forward-looking public action are as important as those for private action. The current national income accounting system provides an example of a perverse economic incentive. Although national income accounts were never intended to function as a measure of the welfare of a nation, in practice that is how they are used. National income per capita is a common metric for evaluating how well off a nation's people are. Yet the current construction of those accounts sends the wrong signals. For instance, the clean-up expenditures associated with the Exxon *Valdez* spill were recorded as an increase in the national income, but no account was taken of the consequent depreciation of the natural environment. Under the current system the accounts make no distinction between growth that is occurring because a country is "cashing in" its natural resource endowment—with a consequent irreversible decline in its value—and sustainable growth, where the value of the endowment remains. Only when suitable corrections are made to these accounts will governments be judged by the appropriate standards.

The power of economic incentives is certainly not inevitably channeled toward the achievement of sustainable growth. Incentives can be misapplied as well as appropriately applied. Tax subsidies to promote cattle ranching on the fragile soil in the Brazilian rainforest stimulated an unsustainable activity that has done irreparable damage to an ecologically significant area. Incentives are such powerful devices for channeling market forces, it is particularly important that they be used judiciously.

We live in an age in which the call for tighter environmental controls intensifies with each new discovery of yet another injury modern society is inflicting on the planet. But resistance to additional controls is also growing with the recognition that compliance with each new set of controls is more expensive than the last. Although economic incentives approaches to environmental control offer no panacea, they frequently do offer a practical way to achieve environmental goals more flexibly and at lower cost than more traditional regulatory approaches. That is a substantial virtue.

24

Notes

1. An excellent discussion on the various definitions of sustainability can be found in John Pezzy, "Economic Analysis of Sustainable Growth and Sustainable Development," Environment Department Working Paper No. 15 (Washington, D.C.: World Bank, 1989).

2. The lessons we have learned from these applications are described in T. H. Tietenberg, "Economic Instruments for Environmental Regulation," *Oxford Review of Economic Policy*, Vol. 6, No. 1, 1990; and Robert W. Hahn, "Economic Prescriptions for Environmental Problems: How the Patient Followed the Doctor's Orders," *Journal of Economic Perspectives*, Vol. 3, No. 2 (Spring 1989): 95–114.

3. In the United States, one company that builds coal-fired electrical generating stations has already contracted to invest in a sufficiently large tree plantation in another country so that the excess carbon dioxide emissions from its newly constructed facility would be absorbed.

4. Because they would receive sufficient financing from the sale of offsets, farmers could be encouraged to plant more erosion-inhibiting trees on highly erodible land, thus promoting two environmental objectives at once.

4

Commentary

Jessica T. Mathews

In an obvious oversimplification, the central global environmental issues for the developing and developed worlds are population and energy, respectively. If we as a global community were to deal satisfactorily with those two issues, we would have touched virtually every one of the environmental concerns that seems to be growing into an ever longer list. The world's population currently stands at 5.2 billion. The United Nations official estimates place the midlevel range—the best guess stabilization level for ultimate global population—at ten billion, about double today's population. A much more recent estimate by the UN Population Fund suggests that along the trend (the fertility rates) that we are currently following we will reach that ten billion as early as 2025 or 2030, and that stabilization will come near the end of the next century at around fourteen billion inhabitants.

There are any number of environmental issues, of which global warming is probably the most important, where there could be a successful outcome, so to speak, at ten billion, but perhaps not at fourteen billion. The choice between those two figures, at what would be considered an acceptable level of individual human welfare—in Herman Daly's terms, an acceptable level of individual consumption of resources and energy—will in effect be made in the next couple of decades, because the momentum of population growth is such that in order to reach a certain stabilization level, choices must be made seventy to seventy-five years in advance.

Herman Daly spoke about the need to change our preanalytic vision. This is a terribly useful and powerful phrase. In the population context it is especially poignant because the history of human experience on this planet has been one in which people have been in short supply. We have now reached the point where exactly the opposite is true. That calls for a change at a preanalytic level that has to be incorporated in an analytic

Jessica T. Mathews is vice president of the World Resources Institute.

sense, in a cultural sense, at a very deep level, and very quickly. Latin America's population is now growing at about 2 percent per year (a doubling time of about thirty-five years). This rate, coupled with its own particular cultural and religious setting, suggests that this issue deserves and demands some serious thought.

We must look again at the underlying assumptions of our entire framework of economics as a social science. What we have is a science that for the most part was created when the view was that the key shortages for economic output were capital and labor. Natural resources, both the supply of inputs and a repository for wastes, were viewed as basically infinite and not limiting factors in economic activity. Obviously, we are now in a very different situation, and that calls for some profound changes. Most important is a thorough revision of the current methodology for calculating GNP, the beacon by which economic policy is made. Environmental issues and concerns will not be solved by environment ministers but by finance ministers and heads of state who will, by the definition of their jobs, be measuring their success by GNP growth.

The current GNP definition does not account for the consumption of resources and therefore blinds members of government to the fact that they are consuming and growing through the one-time consumption of the natural resource base. It is almost as simple as the distinction between spending capital and spending income. If we had an economic accounting system that did not allow individuals to tell the difference between spending income and spending capital, it would become apparent quickly enough. There are many other problems with the definition of GNP, but this is the most urgent change that needs to be made by the United Nations and the World Bank, so that all countries recalculate their GNP in this fashion.

Robert Repetto of the World Resources Institute recently did a case study of Indonesia looking just at three sectors—soil, oil, and timber. He used a rather simple methodology to recalculate GNP to account for the consumption of those resources and found that the real GNP growth, accounting for only those sectors, was roughly half the official Indonesian GNP growth rate in that period. The effects in a heavily resource-consumptive society are enormous.

Senator Wirth touched briefly on the issue of prospecting the Amazon for its biological diversity. This is an important question in the context of Latin America, and one that deserves some attention—not just from those of us who worry about the environment but from political scientists. The rainforests of the world occupy about 7 percent of the land area and hold 50 percent of the species on the planet. They are an extraordinarily rich repository of three billion years of genetic evolution and they are disappearing at the very moment when bioengineering makes it possible to exploit those resources for the first time. This is a tragic irony. The question is: who really owns those genes and who will profit from their conservation? It is a classic problem of the global commons. Genetic diversity is almost never listed as part of the global commons—as are the atmosphere, the oceans, and Antarctica—but it is. Management of the commons and, as Thomas Tietenberg said, concern about the separate issues of who undertakes the protection—that is, who pays, and in this case who might profit—is an issue that has really not been sufficiently addressed.

Another issue was implicit in Dr. Tietenberg's presentation regarding the extremely interesting and creative examples of ways in which the market has been made to work in the public rather than the private interests. What lies behind so many of those examples is the ability to transcend, in the regulatory framework, local, political, and geographic boundaries. In this case we are discussing a domestic context, but in the decades ahead the irrelevance of boundaries in an international sense will become apparent.

One instructive example takes the offset policy that Dr. Tietenberg described into an international context. There are a number of regional agreements in Europe to reduce air pollution. They concern countries that have already undertaken major efforts to improve their air quality, in this case, Sweden. Rather than spending a large amount of money to obtain a 5 percent improvement in its air quality, Sweden would use that amount of money to obtain two or three times as much clean up in Poland's air quality. The reason that it makes sense is that the air pollution in Poland blows over Sweden. Where it takes us in a political sense is toward international political agreements under which rights and responsibilities that we now regard as being solely within the realm of domestic choice instead become international. In a decade or so we will see a set of agreements operating in an international context—some of them regional, some of them continental, and a couple of them global.

That is a pretty hopeful outlook and perhaps one that some would think naive. One of the reasons that I think it is possible is first, of course, the change in public opinion that Senator Wirth mentioned. In a sense the shift that he senses in the US electorate is certainly more advanced in Europe, where the Green parties give political voice to those concerns. There is some evidence that this shift in thinking is at least as strong in many parts of the developing world. The Montreal treaty to control chlorofluorocarbons (CFCs) is the first global agreement to address an environmental problem in advance of recognized damage. The first country to sign the treaty was Mexico. A great number of developing countries have signed it even though virtually all of the contributions to

29

the problem have come from the developed world. This treaty suggests that the North-South division that has blocked developments in the economic sphere might be overcome. Initially environmental in nature, this North-South cooperation may provide a vehicle for the solution of some of the economic problems.

The other reason for hope is that in this moment of political history we are seeing the apparent demise of Marxism, at least as an economic strategy if not as a political one, through a wholesale recognition that capitalism is the more successful economic alternative. At the same time that there is a move toward democratization, we should not confuse freedom and the free market. But certainly there is some congruence there and possibilities have opened up to use one in service of the other at a time when environmental concerns are real and the challenges are enormous.

Discussion

Peter Kahn of the International Trade Commission raised the issue of the level of environmental concerns in the less developed countries (LDCs) given lower incomes and greater need for development. The trade-off between environmental issues and conventional efforts to increase incomes may differ in the LDCs, and gaining their cooperation may require substantial resource transfers that may, in turn, create political problems in the developing world.

Jessica Mathews identified three aspects within the issue raised by Kahn. First, there is a need to eliminate policies that are economically punitive and environmentally counterproductive in order to gain significant environmental improvement. Second, changes that are expected to be expensive may be less so. One example is the Montreal CFC treaty, which will require technology transfer to the LDCs. Although some of this technology will be more expensive, other aspects will be less expensive, so the outcome will be neutral. Third, major shifts in resource and income transfers will be necessary. Mathews predicts that these transfers will come from some type of global carbon tax.[1] Herman Daly added that the question refers to the trade-off between natural and man-made capital. Traditionally seen as substitutes, they are actually complimentary. As examples, a sawmill is useless without trees and a refinery is useless without crude oil.

Thomas Tietenberg then asked Mathews to elaborate on her *Foreign Affairs* article about national security and environmental concerns. Mathews noted that the only growth in budgets throughout the world has been in defense spending, while spending in all other areas has been reduced. There should be substantial reductions in defense budgets by the superpowers. However, the end of the cold war may bring about more Third World conflicts, so it is impossible to predict if there will be a similar reduction in Third World defense budgets.

Elmer Cern, a lobbyist, expressed concern that recent auto emissions legislation would ultimately be defeated due to automobile manufacturers' claims that they are unable to meet the requirements because of the high expense and the fact that the necessary technology does not yet exist. He asked what could be done to convince automobile manufacturers of the importance of this legislation.

Tietenberg responded that the best method is to set deadlines for compliance but allow firms to pay substantial penalties in lieu of meeting these requirements. This will offer the flexibility that previous efforts have lacked. Previous legislation included the provision that failure to meet standards would result in a prohibition against manufacturing a particular model, but this was not a plausible threat. The financial penalties imposed must be significant enough to raise the cost of the car but not so high as to force the company into bankruptcy. Those companies that can meet the standards would be rewarded by virtue of a lower cost product and thus lower prices.

Mathews suggested that the answer to US auto problems lies in the price of gasoline. The United States and Canada are the only industrialized nations with inexpensive gasoline. In fact, gas prices in real terms are equivalent to 1918 levels—essentially at the lowest levels in history. The technology exists to manufacture cars that are more fuel efficient, but as long as gasoline sells for about one dollar per gallon, there is no incentive to build them. Single-passenger automobiles will be relied upon until gas prices rise sufficiently to make mass transportation competitive.

Tietenberg also pointed to improperly established automobile emissions standards as a significant contributor to the problem. Currently, standards are based on a grams-per-mile basis instead of a total emissions ceiling, which means that every new car and every mile driven exacerbates the problem. Mathews concluded the discussion with a graph demonstrating new car registration projections. Because the Third World, especially Asia, will experience a growth in automobile sales, there is a great need for technology transfer to the LDCs from the North where the scientists and technicians capable of addressing the problem reside.

Samuel Wells, deputy director of the Wilson Center and chairman for the session, observed that the problems seem to come from the inability to place values on environmental factors so that they can be incorporated into the policymaking process. He asked Daly if economic analysis could be changed so that new economic models could account for these factors. Daly began by endorsing the bubble concept, as explained by Tietenberg. He pointed out that it is difficult to place values on amounts of air pollution, for example. Instead, he supported determining reasonable numbers for absorption levels using physical science methodology and then allowing the market to determine how the levels can be reached. This method divides the problem into two parts and allows science and the market to work together on a solution.

The United States is given credit for helping to bring about the Montreal CFC treaty, and President Bush was the only Group of Seven leader to bring his chief environmental officer to the Paris Summit; yet the United States is criticized for not doing enough to move the agenda forward on environmental issues at home and abroad, said Roger Stone of the World Wildlife Fund. Mathews responded that the international agenda is no longer based on superpower relations. In that era, the United States was looked to as a leader because it was the world's richest nation. Leadership in the new era will be multilateral, and our role in this new era has not yet been explored. In many areas the United States remains the most scientifically advanced nation; in other cases, our leadership has provoked resentment and perhaps slowed change. What the United States must do is develop a new concept of leadership appropriate to the urgency of the agenda and the new multilateral era in international relations.

Mathews stated that not much has been accomplished as a result of the Paris Summit in terms of substantive policy decisions. She called for a national energy policy, without which other policies regarding air or transportation cannot be established. Mathews stressed that the United States must also clarify its population policy, and asked whether the administration will allow worldwide population growth by linking the question to the domestic abortion issue or if President Bush will recognize the importance of the issue as he did in Congress and the United Nations.

The final two issues of the session were presented by Timothy Atkeson, assistant administrator of the Office of International Activities, US Environmental Protection Agency (EPA), who noted that the world's principal rainforests are in the developing world and that reference had been made to the North-South bargain in which the South will protect the forests in return for compensation from the North. Despite these suggestions, the issue of capital flight from the South remains. If not resolved, the compensation will simply revert to the North as flight capital. Atkeson also picked up on the question of population growth. Hernando De Soto's book, *The Other Path*, seems to glorify unplanned urban sprawl.[2] Although good for the people involved, Atkeson warned that this sprawl is destructive to resources, and decisions must be made regarding the areas to be protected. His comments were designed to point out the other areas that need to be resolved and to posit the question of what should happen next.

Herman Daly responded first to Atkeson's comments. In regard to population, he stressed the class-based nature of the differential birth-rate, in which the poor have more children because economic conditions force them to create additional sources of cheap labor to support the family. He stated that the same factor applies to countries with liberal immigration policies. The interest in cheap labor therefore must be addressed in the population growth context. Daly said that advocating population control is democratic because it spreads the options available from the upper class to the lower class. Too much growth now, he warned, will limit the number of people who can live on the planet in the future.

Daly also suggested that the issue of creditworthiness may require some reinterpretation. Should it include environmental protection or population control efforts? Is a country creditworthy if the surplus is merely converted to more people living at the same level? These are harsh issues that need to be addressed, he emphasized. Flight capital should also be factored into the creditworthiness equation. For example, if all the capital leaves, is the country worthy of credit? Daly called for the redefinition of creditworthiness based on factors beyond the current narrow financial ones.

Finally, Tietenberg responded to the population issue by saying that it was not as complicated as some imply. Control involves convincing people that they want smaller families and then providing them with the ability to meet their objectives. Poverty reduction through the reduction of income inequality can have a substantial effect on the desired number of children. A greater role in development for women and the capacity to limit family size could also have a tremendous effect. South Korea has experienced the largest drop in fertility because all groups have participated in the economic development process. It is important to help those at the bottom, he urged.

The United States has a moral obligation to lead, said Tietenberg. The First World has created the global warming problem that now inhibits the development of the Third World. If the Third World were to follow the First World's model, there would be serious problems. Because we made it impossible for the Third World to follow that path, he said, we are morally obliged to lead the way to a new model. He emphasized the need to begin at home and reminded the group that our approach has been hypocritical; the Amazon must be protected, but it should also be remembered that the United States developed its frontier just as Brazil is doing today.

Notes

Senator Wirth was not present for the discussion portion of the session.

1. A carbon tax refers to a proposed worldwide tax or user fee (similar to

those addressed by Tietenberg) on the expulsion into the atmosphere of carbon derivatives, which contribute to the global warming problem.

2.   Hernando De Soto, *The Other Path: The Invisible Revolution in the Third World* (New York: Harper and Row, 1989).

PART 2

DEFORESTATION:
IMPACT AND ALTERNATIVES

5

Reducing Deforestation in Latin America: The Role of the Inter-American Development Bank

Kari Keipi

The public has become increasingly aware of the environmental changes caused by deforestation in Latin America. A study by the UN Food and Agriculture Organization (FAO) indicated an annual loss of tropical forest cover of approximately 5.6 million hectares between 1981 and 1985, which represented about 0.6 percent of the remaining closed and open forest in the Latin American and Caribbean region at that time.[1] The results of an analysis in the 1989 Tropical Forest Action Plan (financed partially by the Inter-American Development Bank [IDB]) are indicative of the distribution of the major causes of deforestation in the region: advancement of the agricultural frontier, 76 percent; fuelwood consumption, 13 percent; and industrial uses of wood, 11 percent.

Considerable deforestation is linked to the economic crisis facing the Latin American countries. The total net transfer of resources from Latin America to developed countries reached an estimated $35 billion in 1989. In spite of this transfer, estimates suggest that the $410 billion debt will remain unchanged.[2]

In 1989, Latin American per capita GNP levels remain below their 1980 levels and real minimum wages are approximately 90 percent of the 1980 figure. Therefore, the 1980s could be called a lost decade characterized by lagging production, insufficient investments in basic infrastructure, and increases in joblessness and poverty. It is believed that the economic slump has driven millions of landless households back to subsistence farming thus accelerating deforestation.[3]

If the Inter-American Development Bank financed only forestry projects, it would have little direct impact on diminishing the rate of deforestation. In the case of Colombia, for example, addressing all fuelwood consumption and industrial wood use needs would cover only approximately 24 percent of the root causes of deforestation. In general, there are several fundamental explanations for the conversion of forest

Kari Keipi is forestry specialist with the Environmental Protection Division of the Inter-American Development Bank.

land to agriculture. These core reasons, and the efforts of the IDB to attenuate them, are discussed next.

Population pressure and poverty. The increase in population creates a higher demand for goods and services produced with natural resources, and thus the pressures on forest resources and lands are mounting. The IDB does not finance family planning because it is a sensitive religious, ethical, and social issue, but it has adopted a policy of not participating in colonization schemes in tropical forests in order to limit population pressure on these lands. The IDB has targeted over half of its lending for low-income groups, and there is a special provision for soft loans for projects in which the majority of benefits go to the poor in low-income countries. The highly successful IDB Small Projects Program makes funds available in concessionary terms directly to cooperatives, organized communities, microenterprises, and other low income groups.

Insecure land tenure and land speculation. The IDB is financing land tenure regularization and titling programs in several countries. Having title to the land encourages the occupants to take better care of it, thus diminishing possible forced land transfers or speculative sales to cattle ranchers. This, again, could reduce deforestation.

Lack of technology and environmental education. The IDB has funded applied research on forest management and agroforestry techniques that benefit from existing knowledge of the indigenous communities, which tend to be well aware of the environmental value of their resources. For example, forestry and agroforestry extension and environmental education campaigns have been financed in Ecuador, Honduras, and Peru.

Lack of financing for small farmers and misdirected agricultural subsidies. The IDB provides funds for small farmers through the national banking systems of all its member borrowing countries. These loans, which are also available for medium- and large-scale farmers, are conditioned on meeting certain environmental considerations, however. They can be used for soil conservation and improving sustainable agricultural production techniques, but some restrictions apply, especially on the use of agricultural pesticides and the use of credit in areas where deforestation could be occurring. Lack of collateral has been one of the greatest obstacles to financing eligibility. IDB-funded land titling programs can help in this respect by allowing farmers to use the titled land itself as collateral for loans for improved agricultural practices. With proper techniques, such as soil conservation and pasture improvement, the pressure for clearing new lands for agriculture is diminished. Changes in agricultural policies, such as those recently imposed by the government of Brazil when it reduced subsidies for cattle ranching in the Amazon, have been welcomed as important measures to reduce deforestation. The IDB may consider recommending policy considerations in connection with its forthcoming sectoral (nonproject) loans in the region.

Institutional weakness and instability. The IDB has been a major source of financing for the strengthening of forestry and environmental institutions in Latin America, whose importance has increased during the recent financial crisis. IDB-funded investment projects have facilitated a certain stability in periods when governments change but projects must continue.

Short planning horizon. The IDB has financed planning and policy formulation in natural renewable resource management for Latin America. As an example, it has supported Tropical Forestry Action Plans in several countries, including Colombia, the Dominican Republic, and Panama, with planning horizons reaching to the year 2000 and beyond.

Low value of forest to the owner. When the forests have little or no financial value, their resources are often wasted through conversion to other uses. The IDB has supported a number of efforts to increase the commercial value of forests so that they will offer financial benefits to their owners as an incentive to prevent forest destruction.

One effort is the management of natural forests for industrial uses. There are are only a few areas in Latin America where natural forests have been managed, due to the complexity of the tropical forest ecosystems. The Pacific coast of Colombia is one example of successful management of mixed tropical hardwood forests, in which the IDB financed a forest inventory and prefeasibility study for forest management and industrial use of wood (both pulp and lumber). The IDB also has funded management of natural pine forest for industrial uses in Honduras and Nicaragua.

The IDB has also received requests to finance two new projects in community forestry. One would be conducted by an indigenous community in Peru where the sustained forest management scheme was designed partly by the community itself. A second, larger project is under consideration in the Mexican states of Guerrero and Oaxaca, where some 50,000 residents of indigenous forestry-based communities and *ejidos* (villages with cooperative land ownership) would benefit.

41

The IDB has financed several energy plantation projects, but has funded fewer projects for the management of natural forests for energy. One possible project has been identified for the dry forests of the Dominican Republic in the Tropical Forestry Action Plan mentioned earlier. Developing improved technology for wood-burning stoves is another important action that can help slow down the harvest of natural forests as an energy source. A project financed by the IDB in Peru and other projects under preparation for Guatemala and Colombia anticipate the promotion of the use of such stoves.

There are also nonwood uses of natural forests that could increase their value, such as rubber tapping, fruit, medicinal plant collection, other extractive uses, and hunting and fishing. The IDB has financed the development of extractive reserves in the Amazon in connection with a project in Acre, Brazil. Nature-based tourism can also be a benefit, and the IDB is financing the preparation of an investment project for the national parks of Costa Rica.

The IDB has financed research on tropical rainforest ecology and management in Peru and has recently approved a project for Costa Rica with an important forestry research component. It has also financed protected areas in the tropical forests of Bolivia, Brazil, and Ecuador, where protected forests have been established in connection with road-building projects and, in the case of Peru, with regional development programs. The IDB has funded a forest inventory and management plan for the forests of the Bahamas. Other recipient countries of forest or natural resource inventories or monitoring have been Costa Rica, Colombia, Ecuador, and Panama.

The IDB has financed forest plantations covering a combined area of 347,000 hectares through twenty projects in Latin America over the past thirteen years. The projects have included the establishment of agroforestry production systems, forest plantations for industrial and local energy uses, and reforestation for the protection of soil and fauna. Most of the plantations serve combined purposes of production and protection. The IDB favors the use of native species wherever accepted by the local population and when technically and economically feasible. In none of these projects has a plantation been established to replace an existing forest.

Watershed management projects financed by the IDB include actions to conserve and manage renewable natural resources (soil, water, fauna, and flora) in deforested areas. For example, a project approved recently for Ecuador consists of four components: (1) agricultural extension among small farmers for soil conservation and agroforestry production techniques; (2) reforestation; (3) management or exclusion from commercial uses of deteriorated water catchment areas in order to facilitate their natural revegetation; and (4) small-scale civil works for preventing erosion and sedimentation. The IDB has approved grants for the preparation of projects with similar components for Colombia, Guatemala, Honduras, and the Dominican Republic.

The president of the IDB, Enrique Iglesias, declared at the International Environmental Forum of the International Institute for Environment and Development, "The Bank has been called many things in the past. . . . What I would like is that when I leave this institution it can also be called the Bank of the environment."[4] The IDB is training its personnel in environmental matters so that every professional involved in the identification, preparation, and analysis of projects will be able to identify relevant environmental components. An Environmental Protection Division, which would host a pool of natural resource management specialists and ecologists, has been proposed for the IDB. Whether this new unit is created or not, the IDB has already initiated actions to increase the number of personnel in these fields.

Consulting beneficiaries is becoming standard procedure in renewable natural resource management projects. The goal is to promote their participation in the execution of the projects in order to improve the probability that the project will be executed and its goals met. The IDB also seeks to facilitate continuity for environmentally beneficial activities after the execution period. Project costs can be reduced because the beneficiaries could contribute their labor to the reforestation activities of the project. The participation of nongovernmental organizations (NGOs) working with communities at the grassroots level can be extremely useful during both the preparation and execution phases.

The IDB is currently financing the preparation of comprehensive environmental studies in Uruguay, Colombia, and Guatemala. In some cases, recipient countries have requested that the IDB finance proposals to restructure the forest sector institutions as was done recently by the Dominican Republic. Most IDB-funded forest investment projects have included sizable strengthening of the recipient countries' existing institutions. Training programs related to controlling deforestation have benefited groups that have varied from farmers, extension workers, community leaders, and private sector entrepreneurs to government officials.

The IDB administration is working hard to create an atmosphere of cooperation and remove any possible North-South confrontation in environmental matters. The IDB has conducted a number of related meetings and seminars, including a regional forestry conference in 1982 and consultative meetings with public agencies and NGOs on the environment in 1987 and 1989. In addition, President Iglesias and the IDB played a decisive role in the creation of the Latin American Environmental Commission in New York in October 1989.

With rising environmental awareness in Latin America and the Caribbean, ecologically favorable projects should receive sufficient priority from the countries in the region, even given their currently difficult financial situation. The IDB is helping Latin American countries to identify, prepare, and execute renewable natural resource projects that would curb deforestation. Prevention of deforestation requires funding, and the IDB is ready to provide it. As a sign of trust of the institution, its member countries have recently decided to increase its financing capacity from $2 billion this year to more than $5 billion annually during the next four years. All new projects will go through an environmental impact analysis in order to eliminate or mitigate possible negative ecological effects. Good ecology and economy go hand in hand.

Notes

The opinions expressed in this chapter do not necessarily reflect the official position of the Inter-American Development Bank.

1.   United Nations FAO, "An Interim Report on the State of Forest Resources in the Developing Countries," Rome, 1988.

2.   CEPAL News, United Nations Economic Commission for Latin America and the Caribbean, September 1989.

3.   For example, see Robert Repetto, "Testimony on Environment and Development Assistance," submitted to the U.S. Senate Foreign Relations Committee, September 21, 1989.

4.   Remarks made at the International Environmental Forum, International Institute for Environment and Development, Washington, D.C., May 16, 1988.

6

Alternative Rainforest Uses

John O. Browder

Forests cover more than a quarter of the Earth's surface; 27 percent of these forests are found in Latin America. Although many traditional forms of cutting enable tropical forests to recover cleared areas, the large-scale conversion of tropical forests has become one of the most controversial and widely publicized issues of our time. Estimates of the annual rate of tropical forest conversion range from 113,000 square kilometers—an area roughly the size of the state of Oklahoma—to 205,000 square kilometers.[1] Many legitimate concerns are being raised about the long-term environmental impact of extensive tropical forest conversion on biodiversity and species extinction, indigenous human populations, climate, hydrology, and soil conservation. Although the social costs associated with significant human disturbance of tropical forests are by no means precisely understood, there is a rapidly emerging consensus among scientists, economists, and conservationists that present patterns of tropical forest degradation are portentous. Calls throughout the 1980s for concerted international action to manage an unfolding ecological crisis included the UN Food and Agriculture Organization's Tropical Forestry Action Plan.

Underlying the ecological crisis of tropical forest destruction is a dense amalgam of troubling social, economic, and political issues: rural poverty in developing countries, rapid population growth, food and energy deficiency, territorial sovereignty, foreign debt, and misguided modernization policies. The structure of the "deforestation problem" is multidimensional and organic; no single component of the problem exists in total isolation from the others. Tropical deforestation is not just

John O. Browder is assistant professor of urban affairs and planning at Virginia Polytechnic Institute and State University.

an event that sets in motion a chain of devastating ecological consequences. It is also a social process, reflecting a continuum of human responses to diverse and changing economic and political conditions—responses that range from desperate hunger to outright greed.

Responsibility for the deforestation problem and its consequences is not confined to the tropical countries of the Third World alone. Effective control of tropical deforestation requires confrontation of numerous seemingly intractable social ills and injustices that are both country-specific and global in nature. Conservationists and enlightened growth economists face the task of finding long-term human uses of tropical forests that are compatible with the economic development objectives of vastly different countries, and land development strategies capable of reconciling the inherent ecological heterogeneity of the forest with the relatively homogeneous, but often conflicting, economic demands placed upon them by differing social groups.

Development Alternatives for Tropical Forests

There are three basic strategies for tropical forest land use that might link economic development and conservation objectives: plantation forestry, tropical agriculture and agroforestry, and natural forest management.

The Limits of Plantation Forestry

Industrial wood plantations are widely considered to be an essential part of any long-term strategy of sustainable forest resource management in the developing world. Annual timber production rates range from 10 to 20 cubic meters per hectare. There are currently about thirteen million hectares of plantation forests in the developing world (excluding China), seven million of which are found in Latin America. However, by the year 2000 the developing countries will require approximately fifty million hectares of fuelwood plantations, mainly in the arid tropics.[2] The rate of natural forest conversion currently outstrips the rate of forest plantation establishment by ten to one, making the production and long-term supply of wood to meet energy and raw material needs an issue of strategic concern to both conservationists and development economists. In short, many believe that industrial wood plantations, especially in degraded or secondary forest areas, can be used to reduce pressure on natural forests while providing essential energy for industry and households.

Plantation forestry alone, however, like other tropical forest development alternatives, is not a panacea for Third World energy inadequacy. Nor is it always an appropriate vehicle for achieving economic development objectives. Forest plantations tend to obtain maximum efficiency at high levels of output over relatively long production cycles (seven to thirty-five years), thereby precluding extensive participation by smallholders.[3] They are relatively expensive to establish, although they yield a moderate to high rate of return (10 to 20 percent).[4] Employment on forest plantations is usually cyclical, being more intensive in the early stages of seedling growth. Thus the economics of fuelwood production tends to favor large enterprises over small producers, often requires government subsidization, and offers little promise of significantly serving household energy needs.

Plantation forestry has also been considered or undertaken to produce sawlogs, pulpwood, and fuelwood for electrification of small urban areas in various parts of Latin America. These experiences have not yet been systematically studied, but in most cases the hazards facing monocultural tree production include increased probability of fire damage, reduction in biodiversity, depredations of insects and fungi, short-term decline in soil fertility, soil compaction, and weed competition. These environmental dangers combine with high start-up costs, little permanent job creation, and long-term dependency on excessively hybridized or imported plant stock. Thus monocultural tree farming has, at best, a relatively minor role in sustainable forest use strategy.

Tropical Agriculture and Agroforestry

Because most of Latin America's food supply is produced in small traditional farming systems, conservation development initiatives should seek to stabilize rather than replace small farms. Additionally, the majority of the region's economically active population is engaged in smallholder farming. There are between fifty and one hundred million Latin Americans who make their living from farming, a small fraction of whom live and work on tropical rainforest lands. In many cases, these small farms supply most of the food for domestic consumption.

Although Amazonian smallholder farming systems vary, they share several general characteristics. First, they tend to be low-impact systems; that is, they have low capital/output ratios and low-to-moderate use of labor and industrial inputs. Second, production is commercially oriented toward national markets and tends to be limited to a few commercial food crops. Very few forest products are harvested for sale or consumption. Third, colonist farmers often use agronomic knowledge gained in farming different ecological zones—knowledge that is ecologically inap-

47

propriate for the rainforest. Retention and utilization of a natural forest component in farming is, to them, an alien concept. Fourth, these characteristics often reinforce another trait—the sensitivity of smallholders to even minimal exposure to risk. Because risk aversion takes precedence over profit maximization it is difficult to diffuse new agroforestry technology. Finally, unclear land tenure generally discourages smallholder investment in long-term perennial tree-cropping systems. Whereas tree *planting* frequently establishes specific land-use rights in many parts of Africa, tree *removal* usually serves the same function in Amazonia.

There are three main objectives for agricultural development and environmental conservation in most tropical forest areas: increased productivity of agriculture through intensification or increased frequency of cropping; diversification from monoculture to polyculture; and incorporation of productive tree or forest components.

Relatively little attention has been paid to soil management techniques employed by indigenous residents of the Amazon. Recent research suggests that some of these traditional systems are more productive than conventional smallholder agriculture. A comparison of crop yields obtained by the indigenous Kayapó and by smallholder colonists and ranchers in the Brazilian Amazon found that the indigenous farming system produced three times greater yields than the colonist farming system. The difference reflects the fact that the Kayapó recognize many more plant products as crops than do most colonists.

The objective of diversifying crop production is not limited by farm size. In Mexico, for example, small farms ranging from 0.3 to 0.7 hectares are known to produce between thirty-three and fifty-five useful species.[5] Thus farm size alone does not determine farm viability. Smaller farms require intensive management of a more diverse resource base. Short-term yields per unit area in a monoculture will likely exceed the yield of any single crop in a polycultural system but the total useful yield over the long term may be significantly greater in the polycultural system. Research shows that diversified cropping helps to overcome three important limiting factors to tropical agriculture: soil nutrient depletion, weed competition, and plant diseases.

The type of farming system most appropriate to a given area depends on topography, soil and hydrologic factors, access to basic physical infrastructure and consumer markets, and policies that affect market prices for different agricultural products. The key is that a wide range of small-scale agroecosystems exist and tend to share certain characteristics: they produce a wide range of products in a relatively small area, they retain and utilize a significant area of forest, their reliance on natural and locally available sources of fertilizer makes them resource regenerating rather than resource depleting systems, and the sequencing of cropping provides continuity in the supply of food and income. The key issue, therefore, is how to transfer these characteristics successfully to the "modern" smallholders who use resource-depleting monocropping systems on tropical soils.

Natural Forest Management

A wide range of activities, aside from sustained commercial timber harvesting relying on natural regeneration, are now included within natural forest management. Recent research of cultural ecologists suggests that many traditional forms of natural forest management can provide greater financial return on investment of labor than many strictly silvicultural and agricultural activities, provided that they are integrated into larger agrosilvicultural land-use systems or complimented by other small-scale agricultural activities.

One of the best examples of such financial return is seen in northeastern Mexico. A relatively small tropical forest (350,000 hectares) is managed by Huastec Maya and other small farmers. They produce a traditional mix of commercial and subsistence crops (sugar, coffee, maize) through the use of a unique component—the *te'lom*, or natural forest grove. Ninety percent of the more than three hundred plant species found in the *te'lom* are used by the Huastec.[6] Although a *te'lom* alone cannot support a family, its functions within the larger Huastec economy are indispensable. The *te'lom* produces a wide variety of important subsistence goods that would otherwise be expensive or unavailable to farmers, provides nutritionally important additions to the diet (thus preventing the deterioration of diet quality that generally accompanies a shift to commercial agriculture), provides a variety of marketable goods to supplement farm income, supports the production of livestock (often an important source of cash for women), and serves important ecological functions that farmers value by protecting the region's genetic diversity for future generations. The Huastec agroecosystem is capable of sustaining an average family on four hectares of tropical forest land. The potential financial benefits of replicating the Huastec production model are especially impressive. If market prices are applied to nonmonetized production factors, the analysis reveals that the average Huastec household earns a net benefit equivalent to $2,459 per year (in 1987 dollars) from farm production, excluding ecological benefits.[7]

Traditional forest management practices are low-input, highly productive uses that can be practiced on either large or small areas of tropical forest lands; they often are more land efficient (that is, they use less land per capita) than many conventional land uses, even though they are associated with low population densities; they have minimal adverse impacts on ecological stability; and they are characterized by a high rate of resource utilization (up to 80 percent of forest tree species) and a diversity of income sources.

Traditional practices are often integrated with various complementary productive activities that ensure continuity of income flows over time. Where such management is a cooperative venture within a large area, the active participation of the local (often indigenous) population is essential. Such areas are generally found in situations where effective private (or tribal) property rights have long been established and recognized, or where public land-use controls have been effectively enforced.

Although these production systems involve the extraction or cultivation of a variety of products, they frequently are dominated by at least one important cash crop, such as sugar for the Huastec. The financial viability of these production systems is constrained primarily by market distance and secondarily by market acceptance, emphasizing the importance of geographic location and marketing infrastructure (not necessarily roads).

The productive potential of low-impact forest management has been demonstrated, but several questions about the possibility of widespread application of these strategies remain unanswered and should be included in any research agenda for natural forest-management–based conservation and development: How can such technologies be successfully transferred, in whole or in part, from one cultural group to another? If such systems are replicable, can they be deployed at scales of production that significantly increase employment opportunities without depending upon costly subsidies, swamping local consumer markets with minor forest products, or endangering local habitats from overzealous adoption? What are the likely gender implications (household division of labor) associated with transferred technologies? What is the prospective market demand for the commercial goods produced under managed natural forest systems? What support services (credits, marketing, technical extension) and exogenous inputs (fuel, fertilizers, pesticides) would be necessary to ensure stable production of transferred or expanded natural forest management systems? And finally, under what circumstances of land use and tenure are such systems socially acceptable, especially when they entail the restricted use of large areas of forest land?

The application of traditional natural forest management strategies relies largely on restrictive land-use zoning (reserves), often in areas where surrounding land uses are incompatible with intended forest management activities. Under these circumstances, reserves must be treated as one component of a larger land-use strategy that accommodates the competing land uses surrounding them. Low-use-intensity reserves favorable to one group of people undergoing rapid land-use transition may unfairly discriminate against others, resulting in social conflict. "Extractive reserves," in which lands are set aside especially for the harvesting of tree products (e.g., nuts or rubber) but not for tree cutting, can work, but only if cattle ranchers, landless peasants, and other forest land users pressing at the edges are simultaneously incorporated into complementary solutions to their respective needs for land and forest resources.

Conclusions and Recommendations

Tropical forest destruction in Latin America is largely the result of public policies that promote the expansion of commercial agriculture and ranching, as opposed to in Africa and South Asia where the destruction is caused by timber harvesting and rural poverty. No single land-use strategy will successfully harmonize conservation and economic development objectives for the entire Amazon. Different strategies must be adapted to diverse local conditions. These strategies should share three common characteristics: they should be decentralized and their benefits widely distributed; they should be diversified to promote heterogeneity, not homogeneity, of production; and they should focus either on activities that can be adapted to small-scale production or on low-impact activities that can be adapted on a socially acceptable large scale.

Brazilian conservation efforts in particular should consider three important realities. First, between five and seven hundred thousand rural households depend on precarious small-scale short-cycle monocropping for their livelihood; thus, successful development strategies must provide small farmers with the proper technology and financing to incorporate the lessons about continuous cultivation that can be derived from traditional Amazonian agroecological systems. Second, most of the region's population growth is urban based, so joint poverty and environmental development strategies must consider the implication of growing urban demand for food, energy, and building materials on the region's natural resource base. Third, areas of secondary forest growth are becoming increasingly prominent features of the Amazonian landscape. These degraded pastures and abandoned fallows represent an important untapped resource that appropriate strategies should incorporate.

The following conclusions and recommendations for tropical rainforest regions, especially in the Americas, address small-scale farming, plantation forestry, natural forest management, and diversification of production.

51

Small-Scale Farming

Appropriate land-use strategies for small-scale farming should promote (1) expanded low-impact extractive utilization of natural forest remnants on existing productive farm lots; (2) the planting of trees by farmers in conjunction with ground cropping—not only for commercial gain but also planting of those trees that preserve vital ecological functions such as nitrogen fixing; (3) diversification of farm production, especially through the planting of "useful" tree species; and (4) intensification of farm cultivation—continuous cropping with greater reliance on natural fertilizers. Major impediments to all four of these objectives include insecure land tenure, a lack of agroecological knowledge, poorly staffed and underfunded extension institutions with parochial work programs, inadequate technical and ethnological knowledge, and the continued subsidization of monocultural cash cropping and cattle ranching through tax incentives and other governmental policies that promote large-scale forest destruction often to make way for desultory land uses.

More attention must be given to indigenous agroecological knowledge. Obviously, such knowledge must be blended with modern approaches to tropical agriculture and fit existing sociocultural situations. Much indigenous knowledge is culturally esoteric and alien to contemporary commercial farming. Nevertheless, many indigenous practices do show the way toward techniques that may be able to overcome ecological and financial constraints facing agriculture in moist tropical forest areas. Future funding should emphasize the practical management aspects of applying existing indigenous and traditional knowledge at the farm level.

Plantation Forestry

Four potential applications of plantation forestry will continue to receive attention: electrification of small urban areas, urban household firewood production, industrial fuelwood production, and industrial sawn-wood production. Decentralized small-scale tree farming by rural inhabitants in areas surrounding small towns is an income-spreading and ecologically preferable alternative to centralized or monocultural plantations. An important first step toward the adoption of tree-planting strategies in combination with annual cropping would be a localized response to urban-driven demand for fuelwood and sawlogs.

Natural Forest Management

A number of promising strategies for traditional forest management and agroforestry have been largely neglected by donors in land-use planning for Amazonia. Opportunities to utilize more fully the diverse resources of natural forests in conjunction with agriculture need to be further refined, not only as potential development models for extensive protected forest areas but also for application at the small farm level. Additional research is needed on the following issues: (1) the market potential, both local and national, of promising minor forest products and lesser-known timber species; (2) technical production aspects of local industrial processing of marketable forest products, especially minor forest products; (3) marketing requirements for diverse natural forest products (e.g., grouping by general use characteristics); (4) potential uses of different natural forest products as inputs to farm production; (5) financial performance and employment impact of different management procedures that increase yields and minimize damage to natural forest vegetation; and (6) financial analysis of forest management at the farm level and the use of secondary forest growth areas on farm lots for commercial tree planting and agroforestry demonstrations.

Diversification of Production

Diversification of production must become the central and guiding tenet of sustainable tropical forest land use. In one sense, diversity of production runs counter to conventional economic development wisdom advocating specialization around a comparative resource advantage. The reductive conversion of biotically diverse forest communities, supporting tens of thousands of living species for thousands of years, to genetic cesspools capable of supporting one or two commercial species for five or ten years must be rejected as an economic development model. The comparative advantage of tropical forests is their biodiversity.

In those countries where subsidies play a major role in forest land use, the shift from subsidies for commodities to subsidies for biotically diversified land uses should be considered. Instead of rural credit to convert forest land to upland rice fields, policies could entice farmers to productively utilize the biodiversity of the natural forest for financial benefits.

Notes

This chapter is reprinted from: "Development Alternatives for Tropical Rainforests," in *Environment and the Poor: Development Strategies for a Common Agenda*, H. Jeffrey Leonard (ed.). (Washington, D.C.: Overseas Development Council, 1989), pp.111–134.

1. Norman Myers, *The Primary Source* (New York: W. W. Norton and Co.,

1984), p. 2; and "FAO's Tropical Forestry Action Plan," extracted from *Unasylva*, Vol. 38, No. 152 (1988): 40.

2. John Campbell, "The World's Third Forest," *Commonwealth Forestry Review*, Vol. 59, No. 4 (1980): 533.

3. Michael Nelson, *The Development of Tropical Lands* (Baltimore: Johns Hopkins University Press, 1973), p. 155.

4. See John Spears, "Replenishing the World's Forests: Tropical Reforestation—An Achievable Goal?" *Commonwealth Forestry Review*, Vol. 64, No. 4 (1985): 318.

5. Stephen R. Gleissman, "Local Resource Use Systems in the Tropics: Taking Pressure off the Forests," unpublished manuscript, n.d.

6. Janis Alcorn, "An Economic Analysis of Huastec Mayan Forest Management," in John Browder, ed., *Fragile Lands of Latin America: Strategies for Sustainable Management* (Boulder, Colo.: Westview Press, 1989).

7. Ibid.

7

Deforestation: A Brazilian Perspective

Tadeu Valadares

In order to tackle the subject of deforestation in a rational and unemotional way, we must take into consideration a few preliminary facts. In a sense these facts are interconnected with the deplorable phenomenon of uncontrolled and illegal burning of forested areas in the Brazilian Amazon. First, in order to conduct a fair analysis of the problem, the sheer magnitude of the Legal Amazon must be acknowledged. This huge region comprises 60 percent of Brazil—approximately five million square kilometers. The area covered by the humid forest comprises only slightly more than half of this total, 2.8 million square kilometers. Recognition of the geographical extension of this continent within a continent helps one immediately understand the relevance of the Amazon for Brazil. The Amazon basin has an undeniable strategic significance for Brazil's national development. The integration of the Amazon basin into the national political economy is a goal shared by all informed citizens. Thus, how to mix the resources of the Amazon with other facets of the Brazilian economy is a topic of lively discussion. What is agreed upon by all, however, is that Brazil will be truly developed only if rational policies conducive to the optimum use of the resources offered by our tropical forest are devised and implemented immediately.

Approximately eighteen million people live within the boundaries of this gigantic area. This figure includes eight hundred thousand *garimpeiros* (mineral diggers) and less than two hundred thousand Indians. The inhabitants of the Legal Amazon are the manifestation of a larger historical process of population growth that gained momentum in the last two decades. In 1970 the Amazonian population was only 3.6 million, by 1980 the population had reached 7.6 million. The region is still experiencing rapid growth, as significant waves of migrants from other areas of Brazil are attracted there. From a demographic viewpoint, however, the region may be considered underpopulated.

Tadeu Valadares is counselor for the embassy of Brazil in San José, Costa Rica.

The region's economy is characterized by all of the economic and social indicators usually associated with acute underdevelopment. Aside from a fragile urban economy based largely on trade, services, administrative activities, and fledgling industries, the mainstay of Amazonian economic growth continues to be agriculture, cattle raising, mining, and, to a much lesser degree, extractive industries. It is interesting to note that between 1970 and 1985 the number of rural properties increased by 91 percent and the number of cattle herds more than doubled.

The rural economy is characterized by a mix of large and small properties. Smallholders usually practice some kind of subsistence agriculture using a primitive technique, the *coivaras*, which consists of burning trees and secondary vegetation (*capoeiras*) in order to prepare the soil for agricultural use. Although this is a source of deforestation, the *coivaras* have only a minor impact on the deforestation problem. Inacio Rangel, one of Brazil's most respected economists, affirms: "Much of the most terrible devastation we have observed, especially in the Amazon, is not the smallholders' responsibility. It is the result of actions undertaken by large capitalist entrepreneurs." But Rangel emphasizes that the aggressive pattern of behavior displayed by some large agricultural enterprises may change over time as a result of technological progress and applied scientific expertise. On the other hand, the impoverished small producer lacks the financial resources that would enable him to use mechanical equipment and employ modern agronomic techniques and is therefore bound to continue using primitive techniques that invariably affect the environment in a negative way.

The uncontrolled and illegal burning of the forest is a most serious problem. The Brazilian government, civil society, and an absolute majority of public opinion are highly sensitive to the menace created by this vandalism. The indiscriminate burning of the forest irreversibly destroys one of our largest sources of future wealth and potentially endangers the ecological balance of the entire region. Government figures reveal that 200,000 square kilometers of the Legal Amazon were burned in 1987 and 120,000 square kilometers were burned in 1988. The government intends to reduce this to 60,000 square kilometers through new policies, recently enacted legislation, and innovative administrative measures.

How much of the forest has already been destroyed? Some say 12 percent; others say 7 percent. The Brazilian government indicates that the deforested area probably comprises 5 percent of the Legal Amazon. The underlying meaning of these figures is the bleak reality that an enormous area of tropical rainforest is already gone and an irreplaceable amount of wealth, life, and beauty has disappeared. Additionally, this unreasonable havoc produces nearly 4 percent of the carbon dioxide contributing to the greenhouse effect that threatens global ecology. In this context, however, it is important to remember that 85 percent of the greenhouse effect is directly produced by the unbridled consumption of fossil fuels in the advanced industrialized countries.

The Brazilian government's concern with the national environment predates the current situation in which so much of the national and international media is paying close attention to the Amazon. In fact, during the 1930s the first examples of what would today be called "environmental legislation" were adopted in Brazil. The adoption of a water code and mining code, the creation of the National Department of Public Works and Sanitation, and the establishment of the first national park all occurred under Vargas at that time.

During the long military cycle that began in 1964 and lasted until 1985, additional important legislative and administrative measures were undertaken. These included a forest code, established in 1965, a 1967 law on the protection of wildlife, the integration of environmental concerns in the theory and practice of public planning, the creation of a special secretariat on environment in 1973, and the establishment of a national policy on environment in 1981. The measures demonstrate the willingness of Brazilians to address environmental issues irrespective of the character of the dominant political regime.

Nonetheless, it is also true that the environment has never received as extensive or systematic an analysis as the one undertaken by the Sarney administration. At the end of the military regime, the authoritarian model of centralized decisionmaking resulted in an unsuccessful attempt to develop the Amazon, which in turn created an economic disruption compounded by aggressive ecological side effects. In the process of transition from authoritarianism to democracy, the Constituent Assembly drafted a new Bill of Rights. The final text was adopted in October 1988 and one of its most daring innovations is a new chapter that establishes the guidelines for state and society on environmental issues. Article 225 declares that the environment is a common heritage of the Brazilian people and entrusts government and society with the duty to defend and preserve it for present and future generations. Yet the unavoidable gap that exists between theory and practice, constitutional clauses and everyday life, is well known. In order to bridge this gap, President Sarney launched a new environmental offensive.

On October 12, 1988, the "Our Nature" program was presented to the Brazilian people as a new landmark on the long road in pursuit of the ancient dream of incorporating the Amazon into the national economy. This is to be accomplished without the destruction of the Amazonian ecosystem, with deep awareness of past mistakes, and with a critical evaluation of the predatory models followed by today's industrialized countries when they were in the take-off stage of economic development. The main goals of the program are (1) to halt predatory actions against the environment and renewable natural resources; (2) to create an environmental protection system for all of Brazil and specifically for the Amazon; (3) to promote environmental education and public consciousness regarding conservation of the Amazonian environment; (4) to regulate the settlement and exploitation of the Legal Amazon based on territorial planning; and (5) to protect Indian communities, the population living along the rivers, and those involved in sustained exploitation of natural resources.

This long-term effort has already produced a change in policy orientation. The government has created new forests. The Institute on the Environment was created to centralize government action concerning ecological issues, forestry exploitation, fishing, and the protection of ecological systems. A new concept of economic and social development for the Amazon is being designed, allowing for the fact that only 17 percent of the region is effectively suited for economic exploitation and that a new philosophy is needed to combine the ongoing flux of settlers with the economic and ecological potential of the area. We have recognized the need to accelerate agrarian reform in other parts of Brazil in order to diminish the waves of migrants who continue to enter the region. At the same time, Brasília adopted a new policy of giving priority to settlements in the central and western regions, ecologically less fragile than the Amazon.

The government has suspended all fiscal incentives and official credits for livestock and agricultural projects, and also prohibited exportation of timber "in natura." In the coming years the government will make a systematic effort to define areas of permanent preservation and to select microregions particularly appropriate for a range of economic activities. The government will also do whatever is necessary to enforce the law establishing 50 percent of each rural property as a protected site ("legal reserve") in forested areas. By 1995 reforestation is expected to provide 100 percent of wood consumption for all large steel projects like Grande Carajas as an additional means of protecting the rainforest. Protection of the rainforest also entails the establishment of fire prevention and extinction systems, which will be a priority of the "Our Nature" program.

The Brazilian government and civil society have clearly expressed their willingness to cooperate with other countries, international organizations, and interested institutions. In a world that is still, unfortunately, ruled by power politics and in an international arena where hegemonic behavior is an undeniable aspect of superpower strategy, the administration sets only one precondition: in order to be able to cooperate with the Brazilian government in the search for solutions to global environmental problems, all other governments and international organizations must recognize that the Brazilian Amazon is first and foremost Brazilian. When this basic fact is acknowledged by our eventual companions on the road toward an environmentally safer world, the Brazilian people are quite sure that Brazil and the international community will be able to advance the intertwined causes of economic development and sound environmental policies.

8

Commentary

Marc J. Dourojeanni

If we are interested in obtaining goods and providing services through the continued use of the tropical forests, we are speaking of the management of these forests. This can take many forms, including management for biodiversity, for wood, for nonwood products, for tourism, and for wildlife. There is an enormous range of options; nevertheless, management means the manipulation of resources. Even if policy is directed toward keeping the forests, they will not be left untouched.

One of the external factors that affects tropical forests is migration. The people who migrated to the Amazon did so due to a lack of development in the areas in which they lived. Since the days of the conquest, the high Andes were believed to have no value—the high mountains were saturated with population and their carrying capacity had been exceeded; therefore nothing could be done there. As a result of the spread of this message, the population began to migrate to the coast (in the case of Peru, Ecuador, and Colombia), to the big cities, or to the Amazon.

In Brazil, the northeast is viewed in similar fashion. But the true development potential of the Andes or the Brazilian northeast is great. This development could prevent further migration to the Amazon and the cities. The key factor is that the Amazon is directly affected by outside events. It is time to recognize that the Andes, the northeast region of Brazil, and many other regions surrounding the Amazon have a tremendous capacity to support a vibrant population. The much-needed development will require investment. In Peru, for example, more than 90 percent of all investment was devoted to coastal desert irrigation and some roadmaking in the Amazon. No investment was directed toward the Andes, where some 60 percent of the population lives. The Amazon is now paying the price.

Another issue that deserves further attention is education. The

Marc J. Dourojeanni is chief of the Environmental Division of the Inter-American Development Bank.

number of people in the United States who are unaware of the importance of the Amazon is startling. If policymakers lack access to information on the impact of deforestation and on methods of combating the problem, the resultant geopolicy will not properly address the needs of the region. For example, geopolitical views will not take into consideration the potential of nonwood products because their value is unrecognized. This lack of information must be corrected.

Brazil has taken the lead among Latin American countries in pursuing the application of the policy initially called agroecological zoning, but today more accurately known as socioeconomic and ecological zoning. This system is, in fact, what for decades the French have called the *ordination du territoire*. Its purpose is to consider the resource potential of a particular area and to determine the appropriate human activity to be pursued in that area. The principle is not new, but there is an innovation in Brazil: a new kind of legislation to guarantee that the zoning is being applied. This legislation, through economic incentives, governmental services, and infrastructure, will support the most appropriate economic activity for each zone. People will be moved to comply with the zoning as a consequence of their best direct interest and not as a consequence of police and other control actions. Political will to achieve conservation of the forests is indispensable and is now becoming more evident in Latin America and in the Amazonian countries. Nevertheless, these countries are still far from being ready to make hard or unpopular decisions to change public budgets to reflect the cost of conservation. More information and public opinion pressure is needed.

Intensification of land use was addressed previously by John Browder. Less than 50 percent of the cleared land in the Amazon is actually utilized. There are many reasons for this. For example, combating weeds without equipment justifies the opening of new forest areas because that guarantees a two- to three-year weed-free period. In Brazil there is a project under consideration to enrich the *capoeiras* (fallow areas). Peasants would receive incentives for implementing programs of enriching forests with native species in order to reduce the amount of wasted land.

There are many aspects of the agricultural land intensification issue. For example, most of the land used for extensive cattle ranching is not truly suitable for grasslands. It is generally suitable for agriculture and is, in fact, usually the best land available in the Amazon. It is thus important that policies be implemented that promote reconversion of cattle ranchland into agricultural land. Reconversion will allow many more people to earn a good living than under the present land use pattern.

New roads versus better roads does not imply doing nothing about roads in the Amazon, as some suggest. If we want people to live comfortably in the agricultural zones, we need to have a good road system to extract the products and to ensure that they get to market at a competitive price. River transportation also needs to be expanded. The fiscal incentives for inappropriate activities in the Brazilian Amazon have been removed, and that is going to have a very important impact on the future.

It is also important to discuss forest management in the areas that should be maintained as forest. Forest management is not easy, but it is possible and should be done. There are a few successful examples in Latin America, such as the Ticoporo National Forest in Venezuela, which has been sustainably managed for more than forty years. Between the extremes of full deforestation and selective extraction and natural regeneration there are hundreds of options suited to every territory and every ecosystem such that there are no technical reasons not to manage a tropical forest. The explanations for failure to manage are based on social or economic considerations. For instance, people may assume that a forest is abandoned during the thirty- to fifty- year rotation that is necessary to manage a natural forest. There is a need to explain to the local population what managing a forest entails; they must understand and participate.

Brazil has begun to promote extractive reserves as part of its management strategy. The technical knowledge to implement this strategy is derived from rubbertappers and other residents of the forest. The use of indigenous technology makes extractive reserve development extremely promising.

Successful forest management also depends on fair market prices. Tropical timber prices are not high enough for developing countries or enterprises to pay for forest management. Rather than making donations to save tropical forests, importing countries should pay fair prices for tropical timber. This will be a better stimulus to forest management than other options. To obtain better prices also requires organization of the forest products trade for both timber and nonwood products. In the Peruvian Amazon alone, 1,700 species of wood can be used for timber. In each hectare of the forest there may be between 100 and 150 different species. Therefore timber grading and the accumulation of stocks of graded timber such that exportable volumes can be maintained present a major problem. The solution is technologically possible, but the loggers have yet to overcome the organizational problems inherent in creating a grading operation. The waste in logging and forest industries must also be reduced; more than 70 percent of the logs arriving at Amazon sawmills are wasted. The technology exists to avoid such waste.

The lack of clear procedures on how to value forest services (water, clean air, soil protection, genetic resources, reservoirs, and recreation) makes it difficult for policymakers to introduce forestry and especially forest services into planning, national accounting, or even into regional accounting. People frequently blame the economic crisis for deforestation. The economic crisis can, to some extent, accelerate deforestation if more poor people are pushed into the forests. But at the same time, the economic crisis means fewer roads and less infrastructure. So it is not clear that the economic crisis is a promoter of deforestation.

Dr. Browder is correct when he argues that local populations should be served first. Amazonian development plans often promoted the export of coffee, cocoa, meat, or timber, but they did not address the fact that the people of the Amazon need much more common things—things that in Peru are called the *chacra del pobre*. These are the different species of crops that are not marketable but that allow settlers to feed themselves, to have a good quality of life, and to remain in place. With the help of credits, the people must produce a surplus of coffee or cocoa or any other product for export. Proponents of rural development always wanted to begin with the virgin jungle and in a few years export coffee or cocoa. All that requires a transition not unlike asking the first settlers in North America, after the first year of fighting for their lives in the New World, to export tobacco.

Plantation forestry is not a panacea, but I disagree with the generalization that all cultivated forests are environmentally dangerous. I oppose the transformation of natural forests into artificial forests. But in most of the tropical Andes, the exotic plantations are well accepted and are a key element in rural development even in the poorest of communities. It is important not to generalize because there are many places in Latin America and in the Amazon basin where the forests have been extinct for two or three centuries.

In my view, we should intensify agriculture in the tropics as a function of the quality of the soil and of the local economy. Where soil quality is highest, production should be concentrated to the fullest extent possible. The tragedy in the Amazon and in all of Latin America is that every acre of good agricultural land is producing only one-tenth to one-half of its potential. We need to improve agricultural yields. Native or traditional technology should be implemented first, especially because it is not easy to obtain fertilizers and pesticides; but if we can obtain them, they should be used wisely.

Tadeu Valadares reminded us that we sometimes forget the importance of the Amazon for the Amazonian countries. The Amazon comprises 60 percent of Peru's national territory and 50 percent of Bolivia's. There are few inhabitants in these areas, but the administrative consequences are immense for countries that face difficulty even in the areas that are much more developed. Conducting a coherent development program in the Amazon territory is very difficult, especially because people are not informed enough of what the Amazon is and what can indeed be done there. I agree that today Brazil is at the vanguard of the changes—the deforestation of the Brazilian Amazon is much less severe than in the Peruvian, Bolivian, or Ecuadorian Amazon.

The big question is how the entire world can share, in very practical ways, in the responsibility with regard to the Amazon. The Amazon is obviously part of the territory of the Amazonian countries, but the Amazon's fate is the responsibility of all the world. This underlines the urgent need for an open, candid dialogue between the North and the South.

Note

Dr. Dourojeanni's remarks are his own and do not necessarily reflect the views of the Inter-American Development Bank.

Discussion

A question about the potential for economic growth and development in the Amazon drew responses from all of the panelists. Marc Dourojeanni began by explaining that, aside from the agricultural and forestry possibilities, the Amazon also offers minerals and energy, which have yet to be exploited. In fact, agricultural land comprises only a small part of the territory. Land use is necessary so there will be continued deforestation.

Tadeu Valadares highlighted the vast diversity of the Amazon. There are 60,000 species of plants, 2.5 million species of anthropods, 2,000 fish species, 3,000 species of mammals, and 11 percent of Earth's bird life. Of this vast total, only 5,000 species have been biologically classified. Little is known about the Amazon, he said; more than 75 percent of the Amazon has not even been visited by scientists. The region has enormous wealth, and man has discovered perhaps only a tenth of its true potential.

John Browder stated that access to markets is the most severe problem; but building more roads is not the answer because, while necessary, they create conditions for the destruction of the forest. Kari Keipi also discussed the issue of access and use. He noted that in many European countries, the Green parties are working to prohibit the use of tropical timber. In West Germany, for example, tropical timber cannot be used in the construction of public buildings. Keipi identified a contradiction in the goals being considered during the program. He suggested that trying to increase the value of the forest in order to manage it is at cross purposes with usage bans. There is, therefore, a need to determine whether the forest is to be preserved or used rationally.

Valadares was then asked to identify the steps taken by the Brazilian government to reduce deforestation in 1989, how much more they hope to accomplish, and what further steps are being considered. He said that the Brazilian government has suspended fiscal incentives and official credit for large agricultural projects in the Amazon. Additionally, the Brazilian government is trying to enforce forest burning laws and has fined violators heavily—more than $9 million in 1989. These combined efforts will have a short-term impact, but in the long run, Brazil must attempt to increase ecological education. The main problem in this respect is financial. Despite fiscal shortages, Brazil will increase the presence of federal police in the Amazon. The government also intends to obtain additional helicopters to fight forest fires.

Valadares stressed that past results cannot be overlooked. Brazil has reduced the area of deforestation by half. It is impossible to separate environmental protection from the fiscal shortfall of the state. It is difficult for a country like Brazil to do all that could be done due to international economic conditions. Brazil transferred $20 billion to the industrialized countries in 1987, and $22 billion in 1988.

The final question of the session was also directed at Valadares. The speaker asked if Brazil has considered charging fees for resources that had previously been free, given the great potential value of unidentified plant and animal species as well as the amount of oxygen produced by the Amazon. The speaker was suggesting what many others have suggested before—that Brazil could repay its debt through agreements to use the money toward conserving the environment. Valadares responded that this was a good idea but he cautioned that it is a very technical question because it deals with *potential* values. The economic relationships would have to be established first before such a system could be made operational. If the precise wealth could be determined, some sort of system might more easily be created.

Brazil, said Valadares, wishes to engage the industrialized countries in a cooperative effort to preserve the environment. The April 1984 Amazon Declaration stated the willingness to accept international cooperation of countries and multilateral agencies. In May 1989, at the United Nations Environmental Program meeting, the Third World asked for assistance with environmental protection and economic development enhancement, access to scientific information and environmental research, development of environmentally sound technology, creation of technology transfer mechanisms, and financing at concessional terms for environmental protection programs. The industrialized countries should consider these proposals said Valadares. Currently, only the developing nations make such proposals, whereas the industrialized nations are more conservative. Valadares again underlined the burden the debt crisis has placed on Brazilian environmental protection efforts.

Browder also responded to the trade-off question. He said that the suggestion is more symbolic than practical for two reasons. First, Brazil is at greater risk in terms of deforestation than the industrialized world and thus should not need to be bribed into protecting its own environment. Second, assuming that the industrialized nations were affected as much, the industrialized nations would need assurances that this type of arrangement would guarantee conservation. The situation in the Amazon is out of control. Browder expressed doubt that anyone could guarantee conservation in return for large sums of capital. He also doubted that Brazil could achieve its goal of reducing deforestation by half.

The participants were then given the opportunity to make concluding remarks based on the question-and-answer session and the presentations of their colleagues. Transcripts of their comments follow.

Kari Keipi: The question concerning the links between the economic crisis and deforestation is very interesting. Many things contribute to deforestation. If we agree that poverty is one, then a financial crisis exacerbates deforestation because we cannot help people to stay in the areas where they live; as a result, they migrate to forested areas and start deforesting. Additionally, in a financial crisis, governments are less apt to finance environmentally beneficial projects because of the emphasis on trying to export more in order to repay debt.

On the other hand, a financial crisis also means that there will probably be a reduction in subsidies for certain types of activities that might cause deforestation. For example, there would be less financing available for small farmers, so they would have to intensify and also diversify the crops produced in the areas where they live instead of migrating.

Tropical forest action plans have also not been successful because they were created at a very rapid rate. Local communities were not really consulted in the preparation of these plans and no real solutions were found for the needs of the local people.

Tadeau Valadares: One side of the problem is the link between the environment and underdevelopment, which has been discussed extensively from many perspectives and viewpoints. The other side is much more important for the whole planet, and that is the relationship of development, economic maturity, industrially advanced societies, and ecological issues. When only 20 percent of the Earth's population consumes 85 percent of the total energy, something is definitely wrong in terms of humanity and in terms of those societies. These established patterns of consumption cannot be sustained unless the present levels of disequilibria persist on a worldwide scale. In the industrialized world— that is, the centrally planned economies and the market-oriented economies—the consumption of oil, coal, and natural gas is sixteen times greater than the consumption in the underdeveloped countries. The root problems of the environment are thus linked to energy consumption. The biggest and most threatening of all environmental issues is nuclear weapons. The countries that have nuclear weapons may not simply threaten the environment; they may eradicate life on the planet. These same countries have huge chemical weapons arsenals, and this is another facet of the environmental equation.

John Browder: Dr. Dourojeanni mentioned generalizing about plantation forestry. I was referring to tropical lowland rainforests; quite clearly reforestation in the Andean highlands in a plantation context is in many cases totally appropriate.

Indigenous technology is not a panacea—there is no panacea for tropical rainforest destruction—but it has been totally neglected on the research agendas of major agriculture funding institutions. In view of the shred of evidence that we have about its potential utility in achieving sustainable agriculture, we should pay more attention to it than we have.

The rural poor of the Third World, at least in Latin America, are not to be blamed to the extent that they have been for the deforestation that is taking place there. Almost 80 percent of all tropical forest lands are owned by federal and state governments, not by the rural poor. Those governments play a critical role, through their policies and economic models, in determining how those forest lands are used, abused, or neglected. In this respect the Brazilian government's decision to stop issuing new subsidies and credits for cattle ranches in the Legal Amazon is gratifying. However, to my knowledge, this does not prevent the continuation of incentives and subsidies to some 860 cattle ranches in Amazonia that previously received those incentives and are grandfathered under the new benefit arrangement for the next five to ten years. These cattle ranches that have been supported by the Brazilian government have been responsible, by my estimate, for about 30 percent of the deforestation of the Brazilian Amazon. We should emphasize the policy factor more than the poverty factor. The structure of rural poverty and the structure of deforestation problems are very different. We cannot afford to mislead ourselves into believing that if we solve one we can solve the other.

Marc Dourojeanni: I believe that we should recognize that poverty is the direct adjunct of deforestation. Much more land is deforested, even in Brazil, by poor landless people than by rich ranchers. Of course, the poor are not to be blamed. The cause is poverty and poverty is, again, the consequence of a series of policies all over the country, not only in the Amazon. Trade-offs are becoming something to put on the table in the

North-South or in the global bargaining process, and they will form a basis for discussion among many others, such as biodiversity.

Browder: Dourojeanni and I disagree about Brazil, cattle ranching, and peasant agriculture. Brazil has the world's second largest cattle herd; almost one animal unit per human unit, second only to India. All that cattle is not in the Amazon; only a relatively small portion of it is, but it is enough to have done more damage than colonists have. There is no evidence that indicates that an increase in per capita income will lead farmers to be better forest managers—no evidence at all. And if you look at the aerial extent of the damage on Landsat images, for example, much larger areas of the forest have been cleared for cattle pastures than for peasant colonization. Obviously there is the case of Rondonia where there was a program, supported by the World Bank, of concentrated land settlement. Clearly in that case peasant agriculture is the principal culprit.

Joseph Tulchin, director of the Latin American Program and chair for the session, suggested that the panelists were, perhaps appropriately, diplomatic in their presentations and offered a better sense of the disagreements that lie around us in the discussion of this issue during their closing comments. Tulchin observed that the most recent exchanges around the table would have been more obvious and pointed if the Greens policy had been mentioned—the position of the environmentalists, particularly in the North, who in their most extreme formulation would simply deny the the developing nations of the South the right to exploit certain resources that they consider to be the patrimony of the world. Although not presented during the discussion, the position would have highlighted the nature of the debate and the complexity of the issues presented extremely well, particularly with reference to differences in consumption patterns, the difficulties in formulating development strategies in the North and South that allow for maximization of our environment, and protecting the environment. Unhappily, he concluded, none of these issues is as simple as all of us would like.

PART 3

DEBT-FOR-ENVIRONMENT SWAPS: PROS AND CONS

9

Introductory Remarks

Thomas E. Lovejoy

Where did the debt-for-nature concept originate? I may have been fortunate in having been the first person to have at least published the notion in an op-ed piece in _The New York Times_ in 1984. It came to me as I was sitting in a hearing on multinational development agency projects and their effects on the environment. A particularly vociferous man from Brazil spoke about the social inequities that have been caused by various development projects as a result of the international debt and the pressure to generate foreign exchange to pay that debt. As I listened to him, I began to realize that some of the things that we now take for granted—what was happening in Rondonia, for example—could in part be traced back to the pressures that stemmed from the debt. It was not a great leap from there to attempt to create a method of providing some credit against that debt that could do something, in essence, to right the balance.

This was before any debt-equity swap had ever taken place; so because it had not been done even on a commercial basis, the mechanisms were not at all obvious how one might pursue a debt swap. About two years ago, debt-equity swaps became a reality, and they have provided a blueprint for using the leverage resulting from buying debt at a discount in dollars and redeeming it at something approaching face value in local currency. The question became how we could use the revenue from a swap for a socially useful purpose, such as protection of biological diversity, instead of building an automobile factory. One of the important points that needs to be made over and over is that debt-for-nature, or whatever one wants to call it (and there are times when I think that debt-for-nature is an unfortunate term), is no more nor less than a financial instrument, another financial resource that could be applied to problems that would benefit everyone if they were resolved.

Debt-for-nature is easily misinterpreted as some kind of ecological

Thomas E. Lovejoy is assistant secretary for external affairs for the Smithsonian Foundation.

Louisiana Purchase, in which the United States or France will end up owning half the Amazon basin. Debt-for-nature is simply a way to use leverage to gain financial resources for a series of conservation actions that a country would like to see carried out, and it can never work unless it has an indigenous organization propelling it.

One of the points that is frequently raised is the inflationary impact of dumping a large amount of local currency into a local economy. Interestingly enough, that objection seems to be raised far more frequently when it comes to socially useful things like debt-for-nature as opposed to commercial enterprise. It is instructive to note that Chile, the country that has done the most in terms of debt conversion in Latin America, having converted something on the order of seven or eight billion dollars of debt, is also the country that has just about the lowest inflation rate in South America. It is not necessary that inflation follow debt conversion. What has often been adopted as a tactic to avoid inflation has in fact revealed to us a new approach for implementing debt swaps. Frequently the conversion has not been to a local currency, amounting to more or less the face value, but rather to an interest-bearing instrument, a bond or account, in which the capital is not dumped as currency into the local economy. This has presented the opportunity to endow many activities that are sorely needed. You can endow Brazil's National Institute for Amazon Research, you can endow the protection of a particular national park, you can endow a reforestation effort to capture carbon dioxide and help the struggle against the greenhouse effect, you can endow a training institution, you can endow anything that can be endowed and provide institutional stability in situations where so often instability has been more of a problem than a lack of resources per se.

In no way are any of us suggesting that debt-for-nature is the solution to the debt problem; it would be nice, but one could not spend all the international debt in debt-for-nature swaps. It should, however, be a point of principle in every debt restructuring or debt relief negotiation that favorable terms be given to aspects that affect the environment, providing real incentives for countries to harness some of these resources to meet their needs and from which we will benefit as well.

10

A Congressional Perspective

John Edward Porter

The concept of the debt-for-nature swap is generally credited to Thomas Lovejoy, former president of the World Wildlife Fund (WWF) and presently assistant secretary for external affairs at the Smithsonian Institution. I have heard it said that "daring ideas are like chessmen; they may get beaten on the way to winning the game." In 1984, Tom Lovejoy had a daring idea. An idea born out of two crises—crushing Third World debt and environmental destruction. Today, five years and nine debt-swaps later, it is clear that the idea has come of age. I only hope we can win the game.

Debt-for-nature swaps have taken place in Bolivia, Costa Rica, the Philippines, Zambia, Ecuador, and Madagascar. With murders of environmental leaders in the Amazon, surging numbers of environmental refugees, overburdened urban centers, and a forest the size of a football field being destroyed every second of every day, serious consideration has been given to such creative solutions.

While we collectively address the twin crises of debt and deforestation at the moment, we must also be involved in restructuring current development policies in order to preclude the need for crisis management plans in the future. Programs at the multilateral development banks, for example, should establish policies for long-term growth. Past strategies have relied on exports and programs that promote short-term economic gains, flooding world markets and placing an unhealthy emphasis on single-crop agriculture. The result has been rampant inflation, internal disruption, and shelves virtually devoid of all affordable subsistence goods for the average consumer.

Mechanisms to link long-term economic growth and environmental protection are embodied in the Tropical Forest Protection Act, H.R. 1704. The act would use World Bank loans to swap private debt for environmental protection. It also provides for environmental structural

John Edward Porter is a member of the US Congress from Illinois.

adjustment lending and includes incentives to engage local non-governmental organizations in project planning procedures. H.R. 1071 passed the House on October 18, 1989, as part of H.R. 2494 (which, among other things, authorized US contributions to the International Monetary Fund and the Export-Import Bank). The vote was 280–125. The legislation subsequently passed the Senate in November 1989 and was signed into law one month later. Congress's support for debt-for-nature swaps acknowledges the severity of the situation and the desire to effect a solution.

Another encouraging move by the United States was made on August 3, 1989. On that date, I participated in signing the ninth debt-for-nature swap, the first to use US government funds. The mechanics of the swap were as follows: The US Agency for International Development (USAID) contributed $700,000 and the World Wildlife Fund provided $250,000 to purchase more than $2 million of Madagascar's outstanding commercial debt. Madagascar, with a population of ten million and a per capita income of $265 a year, is one of the poorest and most debt-ridden countries in the world. Eighty percent of Madagascar has already been deforested. Human activity has caused the extinction of 33 percent of Madagascar's known primates, and less than 10 percent of the island's natural vegetation remains intact. Yet forest remnants in Madagascar feature the greatest species diversity and endemism in the world today. The Madagascar predicament and the resulting debt-swap is a win-win situation.

The swap, and particularly the use of US funds, furthers my belief that we can continue to offer some relief for entire countries, their ecosystems, and their economies. There are, however, many arguments against the debt-for-nature concept.

There is a premise that economic growth and environmental preservation are inherently at odds. Traditional theories of development have often waged one against the other. The truth of the matter is that there is conflict between short-term growth and environmental preservation. There is, however, a direct and increasingly apparent correlation between long-term growth and the necessity for natural resource base protection. The Brundtland Commission called this concept "sustainable development." Nearly everyone now agrees that this concept—the ability to meet the needs of the present without affecting the ability of future generations to meet their needs—is a good one. Now we are struggling over what the application of the concept means to traditional theories and institutions of development. This effort must be a cooperative one between the developed world and the Third World, and levels of communication and the infrastructures designed to manage North-South interactions must be strengthened.

Debt-for-nature does not translate into debt-for-do-not-touch. The idea that areas will be bordered without benefit to the host country is contrary to what we are trying to accomplish. There is no limit to the creativity that can be applied once the concept is adopted. As we have all recognized the interconnected nature of health, population, poverty, and environmental degradation, we can seek to address the roots of the destruction in developing countries, not just the symptoms. Debt-swap ought to include extractive reserves, conservation education programs, the refurbishing of local research centers, opportunities for ecotourism, and improved health-care facilities. Likewise, projects to match continued need for energy with environmentally friendly, state-of-the-art technologies can be fostered. All of the ideas involve employment and would help create a local incentive to respect the environment.

I have been particularly sympathetic to questions about debtor country sovereignty. Excluding well-intentioned, seemingly misconstrued comments by the press, there is no effort underfoot to "internationalize" the Amazon. We constantly have to dispel this impression. To date, all of the swaps have been performed at the request of the governments and have entailed the participation of local NGOs, not just international NGOs.

Another argument—not against the concept but about its relative effectiveness—is the size of the debt relieved, and the actual amount of land (resources) protected. Debt-for-nature swaps are not a panacea. They are of a more symbolic order. Although I do not support new taxes, if we must have a tax, we should consider a carbon tax. We cannot disguise the facts, nor the percentage of the pollution we bring to bear on the rest of the world. Our national energy policy should reflect our nation's responsibility to the global environment. We should employ increased energy conservation and energy efficiency technologies and bolster support for research and development of alternative clean energy sources such as small-scale hydropower, wind, solar, and geothermal energy. Present hypocrisy must end. It makes our sincerity justifiably questionable.

This summer I wrote to President Bush before the Group of Seven summit in Paris, urging him to place highest priority during discussions on debt-for-nature swaps. The letter was signed by thirty-eight other members of Congress and eleven environmental organizations. Point 38 of the Paris Communiqué, released at the conclusion of the summit, read: "In special cases . . . debt-for-nature swaps can play a useful role in environmental protection."

Up until now, the number one issue on the agenda of the human race has been the question of how man should be governed. That question has been answered: free markets and democracy. Now we are moving toward a consensus on development. Unlike many, I do not believe that economic development means the "end of nature." If humanity is, as some believe, at war with nature, I would like to declare a cease-fire. Debt-for-nature swaps should give us some time to negotiate, because I do not want to win this war.

11

Issues in East-West
Debt-for-Nature Swaps:
The Case of Poland

Richard A. Liroff

Debt-for-nature swaps may shift direction in the future, as existing North-South swaps are joined by East-West swaps. Poland may be the first Eastern bloc country where a swap is executed. The Western partner for such a swap remains uncertain, although Sweden, the Federal Republic of Germany, the Netherlands, and the United States have shown interest. Some of the institutional, programmatic, and financial issues that must be addressed in the context of a debt swap for Poland are examined below. Key questions involve what will be funded, who will be the Polish partner, and at what exchange rate a swap will take place. The sweeping political changes presently occurring in Poland, and the fundamental economic restructuring that must occur, heighten the uncertainty surrounding a swap.

Poland—An Economic and Environmental Disaster Area

The environmental situation in Poland is bleak. As summarized in *The Washington Post*:

> In Poland, regions covering . . . 11 percent of the country's land area and including one-third of the national population were declared environmentally endangered by a comprehensive study by the National Academy of Science. . . . Six million people were said to be living in "environmental disaster areas." . . . Half of the country's total forest area is threatened by air pollution.
>
> Ninety-five percent of the river water in Poland is now unfit for drinking, half of the lakes have been irreversibly contaminated, and more than three-quarters of drinking water sources do not meet official standards of purity, according to Polish scientists. Warsaw and Tirana, Albania, are the only capital cities in Europe that do not treat their

Richard A. Liroff is senior associate for Eastern Europe for the Conservation Foundation.

sewage. Much of the food Poles consume also is contaminated with toxic metals, and milk in some areas of the country has been declared unfit for children under the age of 6.

The environmental problems are particularly severe in the southern industrial region of Silesia, which forms the eastern edge of a vast zone of environmental devastation stretching south into Bohemia in Czechoslovakia and east into East Germany. Lead concentrations in the Silesian soil exceed standards by 150 to 1,900 percent. Concentrations of soot in the air are up to 35 times greater than that judged dangerous to health. Life expectancy in the region is lower than in the rest of Poland and has fallen in recent years, while complications with pregnancies are far above national levels.[1]

But despite the widespread devastation, Poland does maintain a system of national parks, and the "green lung" area in the northeastern part of the country is not heavily industrialized.

Economically, Poland is beset by rampant inflation. The Polish zloty, which is not convertible to Western currency except within Poland, traded at 600 zloty to the US dollar in early April 1989 and at 1,400 zloty to the US dollar in late September 1989. The "gray market" rate readily available and officially permitted in Poland was six times the official rate. Poland owes approximately $40 billion to Western governments and banks.

The Stalinist model of heavy industrialization has been not only an economic failure but an environmental failure as well. Polish industries are grossly inefficient in their use of natural resources and use little or no pollution control equipment. In many cases, industrial technology is outdated by decades. Poland imposes fines and fees on polluters, but these represent a fraction of the cost of abating pollution and, until recently, they were negotiated away in talks between the environmental ministry and other government entities.

Candidate Projects for Debt-for-Nature Swaps

The World Wildlife Fund–US (WWF-US), with which the Conservation Foundation is affiliated, has more experience than any other nongovernmental organization with debt-for-nature swaps. Interest in debt-for-nature swaps has also developed among WWF organizations in other nations, particularly Sweden and the Netherlands, and in the Worldwide Fund for Nature, the Switzerland-based umbrella for the national WWF organizations.

Since 1988, WWF-US and these other organizations have been exploring the prospect of debt-for-nature swaps in Poland. The Polish government has expressed considerable interest in such transactions, which, in Polish parlance, are referred to as "eco-conversion." No agreement has yet been reached on a program of activities to be funded through such trades, although a number of candidates have been cited by the Polish government, Polish nongovernmental organizations, and Swedish interests.

The projects suggested for a Polish debt swap are markedly different in character from those that have been the historic focus of North-South debt swaps. The latter have emphasized habitat, park, and endangered species protection. In Poland, the agenda is much broader. In June 1989, Andrzej Gerhardt, director of the Department for International Cooperation of the Ministry of Environmental Protection and Natural Resources, listed the following activities that might be considered for eco-conversion:[2]

1. Protection of the Vistula River drainage. Seventy percent of Poland is drained by the Vistula, which discharges into the Baltic. Poland estimates that it needs to construct 375 municipal and 445 industrial wastewater treatment plants in the drainage.
2. Coastal zone protection. Poland estimates that 513 treatment plants are needed to protect the Baltic coast, in part to satisfy the Helsinki Convention signed by the nations bordering the Baltic.
3. Desalinization of coal mine waters. Coal mines in the upper reaches of the Vistula and Odra rivers discharge substantial amounts of chlorides and sulfates into these rivers. Poland seeks assistance in developing facilities to recover iodine and bromine from these wastewaters and to use them for production of fertilizers.
4. Reduction of air pollution from local heating sources in Krakow. Krakow, one of Poland's largest cities, is a registered UN Educational, Scientific, and Cultural Organization (UNESCO) world cultural heritage site. Its historic architectural amenities are being degraded by locally generated air pollutants (from combustion of brown coal) and by air pollutants from major industrial facilities upwind. This project would convert two thousand domestic heating systems from coal to gas and electricity.
5. Construction of a fluidized boiler in the Jarorzno II power plant. This would be a pilot installation of a low-emission technology for burning brown coal in the highly industrialized and polluted Katowice area of south central Poland.
6. Flue gas desulfurization in the Turow power plant. A pilot installation on a 200-megawatt power plant in southwestern Poland.
7. Planning of Biebrzanski National Park. The Biebrzanski National

Park project encompasses 557 square kilometers of wetlands along the Biebrza River of northeastern Poland. This is an important breeding and migratory area for birdlife. Funds would be used for planning the park, constructing buildings and other infrastructure components, and maintaining wetlands.

8. Wetland protection—Seven Islands Nature Reservation. Funds would be used to construct dikes and dams to protect a wetland area of international importance.

Thus far, discussion has progressed the furthest on the Vistula River drainage project. WWF-Sweden has expressed particular interest in working cooperatively with Swedish and Polish consultants to develop a plan for managing Vistula River pollution. The Swedish interest is quite understandable: there is a sizable community of Poles living in Sweden, Sweden shares the Baltic with Poland, and Swedish industries would be pleased to supply the equipment needed for effluent treatment. Work has progressed on setting up an administrative office to oversee work in the Vistula, although no debt-for-nature funds per se have been secured for the project.

Outstanding Challenges to Framing a Debt-for-Nature Swap

One challenge to framing a Polish debt-for-nature swap is programmatic. In a number of debt-for-nature swaps conducted by WWF-US, the activities to be covered by the swap have emerged from the long-term involvement of WWF-US with local nongovernmental organizations or government agencies in particular countries. Programs of habitat, park, or species protection have existed to which debt-for-nature funds could be applied. WWF-US has used debt-for-nature swaps to achieve goals shared with nongovernmental organizations or government agencies in debtor nations. It could achieve these goals cost effectively by securing debt for prices of fifty cents on the dollar and less. In Poland, WWF-US does not have such historic involvement, nor do the other WWF national organizations, so agreement on a program of activities must still be reached. As the previous list of candidate projects put forward by the Polish government suggests, the agenda for action may reach far beyond the traditional conservation interests of WWF organizations.

A second challenge is institutional. Debt-for-nature swaps often entail close cooperation between WWF-US and NGOs in the debtor nation with which it has a relatively long-standing relationship. Until recently, Poland has had little tolerance for nongovernmental organizations. A prominent exception is the Polish Ecological Club, founded in 1981, now comprising several thousand members in fifteen chapters across Poland. The club has held conferences and issued critiques of government policies and individual projects. Its activities have led to the shutdown of several polluting industrial facilities. The club has established an enviable reputation, but it depends on volunteers and has no paid staff and no permanent office space.

In the past year, the number of private organizations generally and environmental organizations specifically has proliferated in Poland. Some are established as foundations that may engage in both nonprofit and for-profit activities. A major challenge for the future will be selecting an appropriate partner within Poland to oversee both the administrative and programmatic aspects of debt-for-nature transactions. Many debt-for-nature swaps in the past have been used to enhance the institutional capability of local NGOs. Future deals in Poland could be used in this manner to strengthen the Polish Ecological Club.

A third major challenge is financial. Thus far, the Polish government has indicated that it wishes to have a debt-for-nature transaction occur at the official exchange rate. WWF organizations must decide whether they wish to consummate a transaction for zlotys at a rate that is one-sixth of the rate that, with official blessing, can be readily found within Poland. A debt swap must also be structured to protect against inflation. This might be readily accomplished in Poland, as elsewhere, by indexing to inflation local currency bonds issued in exchange for the hard currency debt. Finally, if debt-for-nature funds are to be used for air and water pollution projects for which some hard currency is needed, creative thinking will be required to encourage the necessary hard currency investments by private parties and the government.

WWF-US will continue to work cooperatively with World Wildlife Fund organizations in other countries and with other parties to facilitate a debt-for-nature swap in Poland. However, many major questions must be answered before such a swap can take place.

Notes

1. "New Breeze in Soviet Bloc is Fouled by Pollution," *The Washington Post*, April 18, 1989.
2. Personal communication.

12

The Brady Plan, World Bank Adjustment Lending, and Conservation Investments in the Developing World

Bruce Rich

I would like to preface the main body of my remarks with an observation that stems from the remarks Congressman Porter made about the real need for the United States to put its own house in order. We preach reduction of greenhouse gases, yet the United States is the single biggest emitter of greenhouse gases in the world. We preach protection of rainforests, but we certainly have a lot to do in Hawaii and Puerto Rico, not to speak of our temperate forests of the Pacific Northwest and Alaska.

A domestic area that requires attention is the gargantuan borrowing appetite of our government in international capital markets. US borrowing has a tremendous impact on the level of debt servicing the developing countries have to pay every year. The unprecedented high interest rates through the 1980s are due, according to many economists, to the US government's need to borrow. Most of the more than one trillion dollar LDC debt is based on adjustable interest rates; thus higher interest rates mean that the LDCs have had to pay tens of billions of dollars more every year on servicing their existing debt than they would have if we had balanced our budget. If there is true concern about the tremendous burden of the debt crisis on the ability of developing countries to deal with their environmental and social crises, intellectual honesty compels all of us to recognize that the one thing the United States can do is simply not borrow so much on international capital markets, thereby lowering international interest rates.

The Brady Plan for Third World debt reduction, the accompanying World Bank and IMF adjustment conditionality that is an integral part of that plan, and the opportunity for increased conservation investments through debt swaps in the developing world are all three inextricably and functionally related issues. Quite clearly the debt crisis and the environmental crisis in the developing world are crises of enormous proportions. So far the record of debt-for-nature swaps has been conceptually promis-

Bruce Rich is director of the International Program of the Environmental Defense Fund.

ing and has resulted in local improvements in certain areas, but in terms of the scope of the Third World's environmental problems, debt-for-nature swaps have made only a small dent. The Brady Plan offers an opportunity for the scope of these swaps to be expanded considerably.

The basic premise behind debt-for-nature swaps is that the urgent need for debt relief in the Third World also presents a unique opportunity to leverage additional domestic investments in those countries for desperately needed environmental and social investments. If one accepts that basic principle then the conclusion is almost inexorable that the Brady Plan and the accompanying World Bank and IMF adjustment conditions should, across the board and systematically, have provisions, incentives, and inducements to insure that a significant part of the debt relief granted to developing countries through the Brady Plan go toward these desperately needed, long-term environmental and social investments.

The basic principle behind the Brady Plan is the essence of simplicity, although obviously its execution is another matter. The idea is that private international creditor banks, mainly US banks, will have an inducement to agree voluntarily to reduce a significant part of their outstanding debt to developing countries if the remaining part of the debt is guaranteed. The guarantees are to come from the World Bank, the IMF, and Japan. There are several important new critical aspects in the Brady Plan. For the first time it involves public international financial institutions—the World Bank and the IMF—in debt relief. Some people characterize the plan as direct taxpayer subsidization not only for debt relief, but for guaranteeing the remaining debt of the private international banks. In talking about the Brady Plan and the roles of the World Bank and the IMF, many argue that the taxpayers of the industrialized countries are directly or indirectly footing at least part of the bill. This is an important point.

The second critical point is that the quid pro quo for the developing countries to obtain this debt relief is that they agree to World Bank and IMF adjustment conditionality. These are the same types of conditions that have been promoted in IMF standby agreements and World Bank structural adjustment loans throughout the 1980s. These conditions, as has been noted and in some cases documented, can have a negative impact on social equity and poverty in developing countries and have tremendous implications, we think, for the management of the environment and natural resources. The thrust, as Congressman Porter and Tom Lovejoy already noted, is that pressure to induce countries to increase exports and reduce domestic expenditures can translate into pressures to short shrift long-term investment in environmental conservation.

A third critical point is that the Brady Plan calls on the World Bank and the IMF to increase their structural adjustment nonproject lending to heavily indebted countries for the specific purpose of debt relief. For the first time the IMF and the World Bank are allowing these countries to use a portion of structural adjustment loans to directly buy back their debt on the secondary markets and retire it.

So what are the implications of all this? For some of the environmental groups that have been following this for several years—the Environmental Defense Fund and the National Wildlife Federation, for example—it is quite clear that the Brady Plan offers, on the one hand, an opportunity to greatly expand the scope of debt to exchanges in developing countries for investments in conservation because of the involvement of the World Bank and the IMF. On the other hand, in its current form the Brady Plan also poses a risk, indeed a threat: if environment and natural resources concerns are not taken into account in the plan and in adjustment conditions of the multilateral banks, then the net effect may be to increase the pressures on developing countries to unsustainably overexploit their resources. That is really the issue at hand.

In the appropriations legislation for foreign operations that must be passed every year, there has been report language and bill language that has addressed these issues. It is interesting to note this because the Treasury Department has not been vigorously implementing some of these provisions even though they have been legislated. In fact, in the latter part of 1987, the fiscal year 1988 foreign operations appropriations bill had specific provisions on two of these areas. One directed the Treasury Department to promote through our executive directors to the multilateral banks and the IMF the requirement that

all country lending strategy policy based loans and adjustment programs contain analyses of the impact of such activities on the natural resources, potential for sustainable development, and protection from land rights of indigenous peoples, promote the establishment of programs of policy based lending to improve natural resources management, environmental quality protection, and biological diversity.[1]

The second provision of that legislation called upon the Treasury Department to conduct a study of the ways in which the World Bank, the IMF, and other multilateral banks could promote and facilitate debt-for-conservation swaps by private organizations using private capital. The Treasury Department prepared this report on debt-for-conservation swaps in April 1988 and, as required by the legislation set out for the remainder of 1988, a timetable for implementation. The legislation required Treasury to identify options and then act on them. The five options that the report identified for the World Bank were the following[2]:

1. The Bank can assist countries in establishing their conservation priorities.
2. The Bank's environmental lending and assistance can be associated and linked, in a complimentary fashion called "piggy backing," with existing debt-for-nature swaps of private organizations so that more resources can be pooled.
3. The Bank can serve as an information clearinghouse and broker in debt-for-nature swaps, for example, in identifying interested private banks and bank syndicates in debtor countries.
4. The Bank should provide incentives for conservation in structural adjustment and sector loans.
5. Most importantly, the Bank should initiate one or more pilot programs in interested countries that would draw on the Bank's expertise. Such a pilot program would include these first four options as well as technical assistance and start-up grants and complimentary loans for tropical protection, among others.

The Treasury Department did not act on this report. It did not push the options very vigorously and nothing happened. It should be noted that all this activity was in direct response to Congressman Porter's original tropical forest protection bill, which caused an unprecedented level of interest in these matters in the Congress and in the Appropriations Committee. In 1987 the Treasury Department opposed the original bill, and the legislation that was passed was a compromise. In 1988 (FY89) the appropriations legislation called upon Treasury to implement the provisions that were in the 1987 legislation. The 1990 fiscal year foreign operations appropriations legislation directs, for the first time, the US director of the IMF to promote environmental reforms within that institution. Specifically, the report calls for the establishment of a procedure to review the environmental and natural resource impacts of the IMF's lending programs and the addition of professionally trained staff, resource economists, ecologists, and poverty experts who are professionally qualified to develop such a procedure.

Finally, the 1990 foreign operations appropriations report language again contains provisions urging the Treasury Department and the World Bank to promote debt-for-nature swaps as an important component of debt relief. The report states that

the [Senate Appropriations] Committee is deeply disappointed by the failure of the World Bank to carry out the recommendations of the U.S. Treasury Department on debt management and conservation. . . . Therefore, the Committee has directed the U.S. Executive Directors of each multilateral financial institution to seek natural resource conservation initiatives as a component of debt reduction strategies, and, with the assistance of the Secretary of State, to seek the support of other donor countries in this effort. These initiatives should include, but are not limited to, debt-for-nature exchanges or the shifting of a larger portion of a lending program to include natural resource protection. Additionally, the Committee has included language in the bill directing the Secretary of the Treasury to incorporate natural resources management initiatives as a key criterion of the Brady Plan.[3]

So far, the Brady Plan is making little progress in promoting significant debt relief and has no environmental provisions. The time is long overdue to carry out the directives of the US Congress to promote both debt relief and associated conservation investments in the developing world on a much larger scale.

Notes

1. 1988 Foreign Operations Appropriations Bill, Public Law 100-202, Section 537 (c).

2. "U.S. Treasury Department Report to Congress on Debt-for-Nature Swaps." Document sent to the Appropriations Committees of the U.S. Congress, April 1, 1988.

3. Report to accompany H.R. 2939, Foreign Operations Export Financing and Related Programs Appropriations Bill, 1990, U.S. Senate Report 101-131, p. 66.

13

Commentary

Thomas E. Lovejoy

It is quite apparent from everything that has been said that this subject is very complex. Environment and economics are intertwined in a variety of ways; I do not think that is terribly surprising. We are at a real moment of truth between ourselves and the total biological system on the planet. It is also a moment of truth between the North and the South and between the rich and the poor. In a sense the debt conversion mechanism can help to resolve these problems. It takes on an extra symbolic value as a consequence. Almost by definition the countries that are saddled with heavy debt are not in a position to do the things they may clearly see they need to do for their environment. I heartily endorse Congressman Porter's very broad definition of what debt conversion for environmental purposes can include. We also are at a point where the federal government is fairly broke as well. Under those circumstances, and until we reach a point where we are more comfortable about turning some guns into butter, debt-for-nature swaps are one of the principal resources we can use in countries that are so driven down by international debt.

I would like to make one minor clarification on something Richard Liroff said. Originally, when we thought about debt-for-nature at the World Wildlife Fund, we saw it as a way to pay for things we wanted to do, projects we had already programmed. But very early on, the ball was taken—and very happily taken—by nationals in the countries involved. Most of these packages have been put together entirely within the country in question, others with some consultation from the point of view of what is likely to sell. Clearly we have to move to an era where debt conversion for these purposes is not solely dependent on the limited working capital of the private conservation organizations of this country. That is what is so heartening about the Madagascar debt swap, where, for the first time, US government dollars, albeit funneled through a

Thomas E. Lovejoy is assistant secretary for external affairs for the Smithsonian Institution.

private conservation organization because it cannot legally be done directly, were used for a debt-for-nature swap.

Discussion

The first question, addressed to Congressman Porter, dealt with the Bush administration's apparent unwillingness to lead in environmental concerns. Elmer Cerin, a lobbyist, offered three examples of this unwillingness: opposition to population control, the Hall-Fields Amendment supported by the Bush administration despite the opposition of EPA Administrator William Reilly, and Bush's refusal to participate in an international conference on global warming. Porter responded that the answer is for environmentally concerned persons to work to change policy. He pointed out President Bush's support of voluntary population control while in Congress and suggested that this has not waned. Porter stressed that we can achieve voluntary family planning, a credible national energy policy, and leadership on global warming if those who are interested make themselves heard. Bruce Rich added that the environmental commitment of some of the other industrialized countries, such as the United Kingdom and Japan, is no better and is sometimes worse than that of the United States.

The ability of USAID to participate in a debt-for-nature swap in Madagascar was questioned by Cynthia Wolloch of the United States Information Agency (USIA). She noted that other agencies would like congressional approval to leverage appropriations, but it is not clear that such approval would be forthcoming or that it would receive public support. Porter responded that the amount leveraged in relation to the total USAID budget was very small; thus the symbolism of the contribution was more significant than the dollar amount. That does not mean that all agencies have carte blanche, but if the amount is small and derived from discretionary funds, Porter suggested that the agency make an effort to use their funds as USAID had. He added that he was unaware of any legal prohibitions and that USIA has a sufficiently broad mission that their discretion should equal that of USAID. He also explained that there was no congressional stamp of approval in the Madagascar case; instead the swap was funded through agency initiative and discretion.

Porter was then asked about support in his district for environmental protection measures. He said that his district was very supportive but he recognized that in some congressional districts it is difficult to support foreign aid of any type while the local economy is in a period of recession. There is no constituency for foreign aid in the United States, with the exception of the Jewish-American communities' support of Israel. People are learning that events in the world can have an effect on them, and leadership is necessary, especially from the executive branch. Environmental issues are receiving more attention and there is no organized opposition to this attention nor to increased financial support. Janet Welsh Brown, senior associate at World Resources Institute and the chair for the session, added that we have an opportunity for international development cooperation now, due to high levels of citizen concern for global environmental problems. We can transfer this concern into better policy, she emphasized.

What type of debt is available for swaps and how the rate is determined was the next topic of discussion. In response to Porter's reminder that debt swaps were not exclusively for land preserves, a request was made for examples of extractive projects that can be funded by debt-for-nature swaps. Thomas Lovejoy responded that most swaps have involved commercial bank debt sold on the secondary market that reflects the perceived possibility of repayment. This does not mean that other types of debt cannot be included, but because multilateral agencies usually lend at significantly better terms, it is the last debt countries are willing to default on. Bruce Rich added that the basic leverage lies in the disparity between the value on the secondary market and face value. Money used to buy back a country's debt can release two to three times as much in local currency for domestic investment and conservation.

In regard to the uses of the swaps, Brown reminded the speaker that there have been only nine swaps thus far. They identified some areas critically important for biodiversity purposes that required protection. The programs that have developed out of this process do not ignore the inhabitants of the regions under protection. In fact, to be successful, the programs must provide a livelihood for the residents of the area. She suggested that there will be a greater emphasis on the development component as these programs continue to grow.

Rich said that one aspect that has received greater visibility is that of extractive reserves. Native populations have lived in the rainforests for years and used their products for export without destroying the forest. The original idea for extractive reserve development came from the Brazilian rubber tappers who became concerned in the mid-1980s about deforestation through large-scale road building and agricultural colonization. They felt that extractive production could be intensified. Studies in Guatemala and Indonesia reinforce the viability of this proposal. Extractive reserves represent an alternative form of conservation investment that debt-for-nature swaps could incorporate. Money could be directed, for example, to the rubber tappers' organization in Brazil or to the chicle farmers of Guatemala to promote development that does not destroy the resource base.

Axel Peuker of the World Bank posed three related questions. The first involved the trade-off between environmental protection and poverty reduction. He cited tapping water reserves versus preserving them as a concrete example of this conflict. Peuker asked how much of this is reflected in debt swaps, and also asked about the size of the swaps in terms of their ability to make an impact. He also wondered if there have been any efforts to include environmental conditionality in loans so that both countries and multilateral lenders will be required to address ecological issues when designing major lending projects.

Lovejoy responded that swaps are small now but there is no reason for them to remain so. Swaps represent resources that, for a conservation organization, are not trivial. Even if debt-for-nature swaps reach the level they should, he continued, they will not be able to solve the problem alone. The attraction of the debt swaps is that they are being used to an extent that approximates the severity of the problem. Rich agreed and added that the Brady Plan's massive debt reduction program and the involvement of the IMF and the World Bank as the key facilitators, catalysts, and even guarantors presents a unique opportunity to increase the size of the swaps.

In regard to conditionality, Rich said that because countries receive credit from the multilaterals by meeting certain conditions, it is essential that they contain conditions on the environment, natural resource management, and inducements for long-term investment in the environment and in desperately needed social investment. The concept of debt-for-nature, he concluded, can be used to finance anything, so groups concerned with poverty levels could use the same principle to promote poverty reduction.

Brown reported that the World Resources Institute had found that the worst poverty and the worst environmental conditions occur in the same areas. The poor pay for poor environmental practices and sometimes these practices can be costly. The once-emphasized dichotomy between economic development and environmental protection has been replaced by a recognition that societies cannot sacrifice one component for the other. As a result, environmental and social welfare groups no longer perceive themselves as rivals.

The World Bank and the IMF have been criticized by social and church groups due to the poverty-inducing effects of some of their proscribed structural adjustment programs, observed Rich. UN agencies have critiqued the World Bank and IMF programs, blaming them for the starvation of millions. The IMF itself has studied the implications of its policies and admitted that some people are worse off in the short term. The World Bank's 1987 Development Committee report, "Environment, Growth and Adjustment," identified links with poverty and the environment by arguing that poverty pushes people to use resources faster than they can be replaced. Richard Liroff added that WWF-US has a program called "Wildlands and Human Needs," which recognizes that environmental needs cannot be considered without taking into account the needs of indigenous peoples. Other groups have similar thinking, he said.

Ruben Pascual, agricultural attaché of the Philippine embassy, offered a Third World perspective on the debt-for-nature issue. He observed that Porter was correct in stressing that the sensitivities of the Third World must be recognized. He cautioned that a campaign for environmental protection must consider the economic needs of the population as well. For example, Polish workers may prefer jobs to clean air for their children. Unless the United States can create programs to put more money into workers' pockets, he said, some workers will not place a high priority on breathing clean air. Pascual further suggested that Brazil's concern for the Amazon may be economically motivated by the need to obtain debt relief. In most developing countries, environmental protection has not been made the top priority because the need to feed the population has not been met, he explained.

Liroff agreed with Pascual's interpretation and asserted that environmental protection will be a part of Poland's economic restructuring. The vast number of inefficient facilities creates the potential for political conflict within Solidarity's labor base. Fragmentation is conceivable and environmental protection may not receive sufficient support. It is vitally important, he emphasized, that the United States and Western Europe help Poland during this transition.

The motivation for involvement in the environmental movement is the desire to improve the quality of life, said Brown. Hunger must be addressed first, as part of saving the environment is creating programs for health, food, and shelter, which are as important as agricultural reform or promoting new techniques. Brown cautioned against the jobs-versus-environment argument, which has been used in the United States in the past. Several studies have documented that the number of jobs created by the environmental movement exceeds by a wide margin the number of jobs lost. Liroff added that what makes good environmental sense often makes good economic sense as well. Poland is full of inefficiency and many of its industrial plants should be closed if Poland truly wants to establish an effective market economy.

The final comments were directly related to the question of trade-offs. It is useful to separate nature and development in our objectives, argued one participant. It is said that the poor will always be with us, yet the same cannot be said of the environment. The real value in distinguishing between debt-for-nature swaps and structural adjustment lending is that the debt-for-nature swap can buy time until a longer-term solution to the environmental crisis is found. The speaker did not see the two programs in conflict but felt that they should be separated.

Rich disagreed vehemently with aspects of this comment. Although he agreed that various elements must be distinguished, he counseled that the whole picture cannot be ignored. It is counterproductive to use debt-for-nature to set aside postage-stamp-sized areas of protected land while IMF and World Bank loans pour in and encourage the use of natural resources at an unsustainable rate. Rich stressed that the role of the multilateral agencies in influencing policy must be considered, which means analyzing how economic resources are targeted in various countries and what happens to the environment. The World Bank has produced some essays to demonstrate the connections between macro-economic adjustment policies and conditions tied to structural adjustment loans and the impact and implications for forest and natural resource management. Debt-for-nature swaps are discreet, but if we ignore the larger picture, they are worthless, he said. The money and power are directed at structural adjustment policies, which can have adverse environmental consequences.

Note

Congressman Porter was present for only the first three questions of the session. Thomas Lovejoy was also unable to stay for the entire period.

PART 4

AIR POLLUTION CONTROL AND ECONOMIC DEVELOPMENT

14

Mexico City's Program to Reduce Air Pollution

Fernando Menéndez Garza

Geography, Economy, and Pollution

The metropolitan area of Mexico City consists of more than two thousand square kilometers, comprising the Federal District and seventeen towns in the state of Mexico, with a population of 19.5 million. Mexico City is located at approximately 2,300 meters above sea level at a tropical latitude of 19.5 degrees North. It is confined within a deep valley naturally encircled by a great chain of mountains, all of volcanic origin. These physical and geographical characteristics create a natural isolation and contribute to frequent thermal inversions and atmospheric depressions, especially during the winter, presenting an impediment to the development of air currents over prolonged periods of time; the lack of winds impedes the dispersion of pollutants.

The enclosed valley of Mexico, where the metropolitan area of Mexico City is located, suffers from severe hydrological and ecological damage. Almost 75 percent of its coniferous and oak forests have disappeared and almost 99 percent of its lakes have dried up. A little more than 70 percent of its rural lands show an advanced state of erosion; large amounts of suspended dust particles in the atmosphere during windy days are attributable to the total lack of vegetation in these areas.

For various historic and economic reasons, the metropolitan area of Mexico City has become an urban, economic, and political concentration with few precedents in the world. Its growth has been extraordinarily rapid in the past three decades due to the economic opportunities it offers, a fast natural population increase, and continuous immigration from rural areas. The metropolitan area (which represents only one-thousandth of the total Mexican territory) contains 25 percent of the national population, and is still growing at 5 percent per year, almost two times the national average. The metropolitan area of Mexico City

Fernando Menéndez Garza is coordinator of the Program to Control Atmospheric Contamination of the Government of Mexico City.

generates 36 percent of the gross national product and consumes nearly 25 percent of the total energy of the country, primarily as hydrocarbons burned by a broad spectrum of transportation, manufacturing, and service industries. All of these factors contribute to its atmospheric pollution problem.

More than 2.5 million vehicles consume approximately fourteen million liters of gasoline and four million liters of diesel fuel per day, while close to thirty thousand manufacturing and service industries and two energy generating plants burn approximately thirty-two thousand barrels of fuel oil and more than two hundred million cubic feet of gas. The resultant emissions combine to interact in a photochemical process with hundreds of tons of suspended particles that the wind brings from the deforested, dried up, or eroded zones that surround the city. For this reason, throughout the year air quality levels in Mexico City normally exceed standard levels (similar to those in other countries), causing decreased visibility and threatening public health.

Trends

After ten years of positive fiscal, economic, and regulatory stimulus and penalties to induce decentralization, with increasingly successful results, it is predicted that the city will continue to grow at relatively fast rates. This growth could bring, among other consequences, a larger consumption of energy and continued ecological damage to the metropolitan area of Mexico City due to the following factors: (1) the population growth, which increases at an annual rate of 5 percent; (2) the number of vehicles circulating, which increases at an annual rate of 4 percent; (3) the number of trips per person per day, which grows with the population, new lifestyles, and economic activity; (4) the kilometers driven per vehicle, which grow based on the above-mentioned items plus the expansion of the urban area and the reduction of average driving speed; (5) the continuous expansion of the urban area over forested zones, which grows between 4 and 5 percent a year; (6) the existing extent of deforestation and soil erosion; and (7) the ever-increasing volume and intensity of the consumption of goods and services, which thrives on additional economic activity, population growth, and new consumer habits.

Basis for an Action Program

Only recently were the real meaning and implications of the atmospheric pollution problem understood. In March 1988, the General Law of

Ecological Balance and Environmental Protection became effective as an integrated legislative response to the environmental problems of the country. The law establishes a broad system of mutual assistance among the federal government, federal entities, and municipalities, decentralizing resources and responsibilities under a coordinated and cooperative framework. Article 6 of the law grants authority to states and municipalities for the prevention and control of atmospheric pollution generated by sources in their jurisdiction. Article 9 of the law also grants the Mexico City government authority to regulate mobile sources and emissions from businesses and services, parking lot inspections, vehicle traffic management, control over transportation systems and public roads, emission regulations for public transportation, and authority over urban development and land use. The federal regulatory agency has reserved to itself control over industrial sources, determination of technical regulations, and operation of atmospheric monitoring systems.

The law makes available a repertory of ecological policy instruments of broad coverage and applicability, strong enough to support an integrated planning process comprising the federal government, the federal entities, municipalities, and society itself. This includes the ecological organization of regions and human settlements, the mandatory evaluation of environmental impacts of important projects, ecological planning regulations, steps for the protection of natural areas, research and education, inspection, and mechanisms for social participation.

In this context, the president of Mexico has decided to approach the problem decisively, engaging the highest political will, in order to contain the deteriorating trend of the quality of Mexico City's air. At his inauguration ceremony on December 1, 1988, he clearly instructed the federal district government to assume the commitment of combating atmospheric pollution in Mexico City. His instructions were unequivocal: "I am giving precise, urgent and strict instructions to the mayor of the federal district to start working immediately, with effective actions and encouraging community participation, in the fight against pollution."

Program Description

During the next five years a series of measures will be adopted in transportation systems, in energy generation, in manufacturing and service industries, and in urban and rural zones surrounding the metropolitan area of Mexico City. These measures will include one or more of the following actions:

Improved fuel quality. The construction of refineries will allow us to offer the necessary volume of high quality lead-free gasoline that will be required by vehicles fitted with catalytic converters, as well as the fuel and oxygenated additives that will allow efficient combustion processes at the high altitude of Mexico City. We will also begin the construction of desulfurization plants to produce low-sulfur diesel and fuel oils.

Change of highly polluting fuels for clean burning ones. We are starting a fuel oil substitution for natural gas in power generating plants and the ten most highly polluting industries. We are also substituting liquefied petroleum gas for leaded gasoline in 45,000 in-city cargo trucks.

Installation of new systems for combustion and emissions control in vehicles, in manufacturing and in service industries. Annual automobile inspections are now required and are performed in public service stations as well as in private workshops. We anticipate strengthening this requirement and shortening the period for inspections to every six months. Industries are now subject to constant inspections and will be required to install scrubbers and particle control systems. We will start mandatory inspection and control of diesel vehicles. We have begun the renovation of urban bus fleets, the installation of new engines, and an adequate diesel motor maintenance program to reduce pollution and expand public transportation services. We will begin a program for retrofitting three-way catalytic converters in public service vehicles.

Rationalization and restructuring of transportation activities. We are considering the following actions: mechanisms to restrict circulation of all private vehicles one day a week during the winter; establishment of a corresponding system of incentives and penalties through higher prices for fuel and parking; removal from circulation of all vehicles found polluting excessively; prohibition of parking lots in specific zones as a disincentive and means of alleviating traffic congestion and increasing average speed; incentives for shared use of vehicles; restrictions to traffic in specific areas and at specific times; regulation and encouragement of institutional transportation; reconfiguration and freeing of roadways and lanes for the exclusive use of buses; establishment of continuous working hours in public sector offices to reduce the volume of trips per person; and an increase in traffic police for adequate enforcement of these actions.

Ecological restoration of areas from which the wind brings suspended particles. This program will involve the establishment of permanent vegetation cover through extensive reforestation, grass planting, water recovery, agriculture and livestock revitalization activities, and paving of streets.

These policies were selected because they have already undergone experimentation in other countries (as well as in Mexico), have been widely applied, and their effectiveness has been proven. They imply the use of technologies that are commercially available, and the energy they require is available at a reasonable cost. They require adjustment in urban lifestyles and in institutional activities that can be accomplished in a short period, and they have a significant reduction effect on total emissions and on one or more of the major pollutants. Their relative cost effectiveness is also significant.

15

The Possibilities and Limits of Environmental Protection in Mexico

—————— *Richard A. Nuccio* ——————

The origins of Mexico's acute contemporary political and economic crises lie in the 1960s. It was during that decade that the economic model of import-substitution industrialization being followed by Mexico gave early indicators of having exhausted its usefulness. Part of the inadequacy of the model lay in its neglect of the rural areas, where the majority of Mexicans at one point lived and where productive activities might have helped feed Mexico's increasing numbers and slowed the rush of population to the cities.

Another part lay in an intrinsic failure of the model everywhere it was applied in Latin America: the creation of an inefficient industrial structure that produced low-quality goods competitive only in an internal market protected by high tariffs. This model led to the dead end in Mexico, as in many countries, of substituting imports of even more expensive capital goods and, at times, raw materials for the earlier imports of finished and intermediate goods. Poor-quality products, desirable only in the protected domestic market, never earned the foreign exchange as exports to pay for the imports of capital goods. Foreign borrowing became the only way to fill the resulting foreign exchange gap.

Moreover, only the relatively privileged upper and middle classes could afford Mexican-produced, high-priced luxuries such as stoves, washers and dryers, and refrigerators. This small market of wealthier Mexicans, constituting perhaps 15 percent of the population, lived in the major cities. A vicious cycle began. Protected industries located close to their major markets in the cities drew labor from the countryside into increasingly crowded urban centers. Government policies kept agricultural prices low to supply inexpensive foodstuffs to the urban working class. Low agricultural prices drove even more peasants into urban areas and producers out of basic commodities such as beans and corn and into

Richard A. Nuccio is adjunct professor at Georgetown University and senior associate of the Inter-American Dialogue.

cash crops for exports.

The environmental consequences were equally grave. Guadalajara, Monterrey, Puebla, and, above all, Mexico City became the primary poles of economic growth and of environmental deterioration. A macro-cephalic development that outstripped urban services of housing, potable water, and sewage and other waste disposal became the rule. Industrial discharges and the overwhelming number of dangerous but previously isolated sites of chemical production and energy distribution by residential areas contributed to truly horrific environmental conditions. It is this pattern of development that Mexico must now, in the midst of severe austerity, try to reorient.

The environmental and resource consequences of Mexico's development did not happen by accident. They flowed from a pattern of economic growth that was presented as being technically sound at the time—perhaps because it was politically acceptable to a growing middle class. But that model of development has already seriously eroded the human and material base upon which the future of Mexico will be built. In response to the economic and environmental failures of this import-substitution model, a new model of export-led growth has been adopted by Mexico.[1] But the resumption of growth in Mexico without an examination of the style of development followed in the past and its environmental consequences may leave Mexico less equipped in the future to deal with the powerful social, economic, and political challenges it will face in the next century, less than a decade away.

Subordinating Agriculture to Industry

Under Mexico's import-substitution industrialization, the modernization of agriculture was sought through the investment of public funds in capital-intensive technologies suitable for good farmland or areas brought under cultivation by large irrigation projects. By the 1970s a pattern of agricultural production in Mexico had emerged that is at the root of Mexico's urban environmental dilemmas. As technology facilitated the exportation of manufacturing and of advanced labor processes worldwide, a "globalization" of production occurred. For Mexican agriculture, this meant a new mode of production characterized by the commercial contracting and technological packaging of whole-crops industries such as strawberries, asparagus, cucumbers, and tomatoes. Agribusiness giants like Del Monte, General Foods, and Campbell's, other food brokers, and contracting supermarket chains such as Safeway brought Mexico into the global supermarket.

The reduction of agriculture to the "adjunct of industry" and the internationalization of agribusiness to the production of exportable fruits and vegetables and of feedgrains contributed to Mexico's crisis of the 1980s. Despite the supposed benefits of comparative advantage theory, Mexico's agricultural exports have not kept pace with the costs of increasing imports of other agricultural commodities made necessary by this very model of agricultural development. In a pattern not unlike that of manufactures, the prices of crops such as grains and soybeans sold predominantly by industrial countries have risen faster than the prices of commodities exported by developing countries. In addition, agribusiness has failed to absorb rural labor displaced by modernization and industrialization and to improve the nutritional standards of the mass of the population.[2]

The "catch-22" of Mexico's current agricultural dilemma is well illustrated by the $5 billion program to spur food production announced in mid-1985 by President de la Madrid. The impetus for the program was a food import bill for 1985 of $1.5 billion—to be paid with scarce foreign exchange—to import corn and other daily dietary staples once grown in sufficient quantities in Mexico. Kenneth Shwedel, a senior economist at Banamex, a major Mexican bank, commented to the *Wall Street Journal*, "Today's food problem comes, in part, from the success of the urbanization of the 1950s and 1960s. Real agricultural prices all reached a peak in 1950 and have been falling ever since."[3] In making agriculture the adjunct of industry, the Mexican government held down the price of tortillas to feed the thousands of people from the countryside drawn to industrial jobs in the cities. This depressed prices for corn, driving even more rural inhabitants off the land and into the cities, where industrial employment could not keep up with the expanding demand for work.

While the government controlled the corn market, a private sorghum market sprouted. Land planted to sorghum (primarily used as feedgrain for dairy cattle raised in Mexico) rose from 1 million hectares to 1.5 million hectares between 1970 and 1980. Corn cultivation, on the other hand, declined from 7.3 million to 6.9 million hectares. From 1958 to 1980, the production of sorghum grew 2,772 percent, and the amount of land sown in sorghum climbed 1,300 percent.[4]

At a time of heavy indebtedness, Mexico hardly needs a $5 billion program that will add to the public deficit because its product—corn—will be sold at controlled prices to lower the cost of tortillas. But any attempt to raise tortilla prices to provide greater incentives for corn producers could provoke urban protests that Mexico must also seek to avoid.

Unfortunately, Mexico's food import bill continues to rise. In the first three months of 1989, agricultural imports more than doubled, to $482.3 million from $225.2 million in the first quarter of 1988. It is estimated that the food import bill for 1989 will be more than $3 billion, or twice the 1985 bill that spurred former President de la Madrid's program for agriculture. In response, President Salinas launched a series of sweeping measures to immediately revive agricultural production in late August 1989.[5]

Mexico City, Contamination Central

The Metropolitan Zone of Mexico City (MZMC) is the center of Mexico's most important economic, political, and cultural activities.[6] A product of unplanned urban growth, the city contains almost 25 percent of the national population, provides 42 percent of all jobs, generates 53 percent of wages and salaries in the country, includes 38 percent of the total value of industrial plants, accounts for 49 percent of sales of durable goods, and receives 55 percent of public investment in social welfare. The city and the metropolitan area consume 40 percent of the total food production, buy 90 percent of all electrical appliances, use 66 percent of the country's energy and telephones, and purchase 58 percent of the automobiles on the country's highways.[7]

Between 1970 and 1980, the Federal District grew at a 4.5 percent annual rate, and surrounding metropolitan municipalities grew at a rate of 10 percent. Over the last ten years, 270,000 people arrived in the city annually, attracted by the hope of economic opportunity and driven from the countryside by declining employment in the agricultural sector. This population increase and natural growth have combined to produce one of the largest cities on Earth: 18 million inhabitants by 1989 (10.3 million in the Federal District and another 7.7 in the state of Mexico) in an area of approximately 1,250 square kilometers.[8]

The outcome of a policy of centralized growth, Mexico City has become the place in which the majority of the natural and artificial sources of contamination are concentrated: erosion; exposed trash and feces; entry into the subsoil of untreated water; emissions from factories, workshops, thermoelectric plants, refineries, petrochemical plants, cement and fertilizer plants, iron and steel foundries, and a large quantity of industrial and domestic incinerators; and millions of internal combustion vehicles and airplanes. Together, these sources spew approximately six thousand tons of contaminants into the atmosphere daily.

Indiscriminate dumping of domestic and industrial liquid waste into lakes and rivers and along shorelines has led to a significant contamination of above-ground and subterranean waters. Approximately 50 cubic meters per second of residual waters are dumped, and only 70 percent is filtered by the sewage system. In the past few years, the degradation of important ecosystems has worsened. For example, Lake Guadalupe (the closest lake to the Federal District) has become extremely polluted. Surrounded a few years ago by more than 2,800 hectares of farmland, today this lake is considered one huge septic tank. It receives nearly 30 million cubic meters of residual waters annually, which come principally from industrial and residential areas close to the dam. These discharges contain garbage, grease, detergents, and phosphates. Almost all the waste waters generated in neighboring residential areas enter the lake without any treatment.[9]

Excessive water consumption in the MZMC has already produced serious ecological imbalances in the water table of the region. Overuse of water has caused terrain in various zones of the Mexico Valley to sink. In Xochimilco-Tulyehualco, the land has sunk 4 meters in less than twenty years.[10]

To compensate for the indiscriminate extraction of drinkable water, one of the policies followed by the authorities is the substitution of treated residual water. Recycling of this water has been the only available alternative for area farmers to maintain the use of their lands. Unfortunately, studies have shown that the utilization of treated waste water for cultivation eventually causes sterility of the soil because of the high concentration of salts and heavy metals in the treated water.[11] In addition, some agricultural products grown with this treated water are highly noxious because they contain toxic elements affecting human health. Several studies have confirmed that residual waters in the Mexico Valley contain some forty pathogenic microorganisms that are very resistant to water treatment and to drugs taken by humans infected by them.[12]

The costs of expanding Mexico City's water supplies are becoming prohibitive. In the 1990s, increasing the supply will require bringing water from sources some 200 kilometers away and almost 2,000 meters lower than the altitude of the city. Such a feat would take nearly 125 trillion kilojoules of electrical energy each year and require construction of six 1,000-megawatt power plants at a cost of $6 billion. The city is thus faced with three rising costs in obtaining water: increasing distance of water transport, increasing height of water lift, and rising energy costs.[13] In addition, the new power plants, like all fossil-fueled ones, will contribute to the greenhouse warming effect and, depending on the technology, to other environmental effects downwind.

Atmospheric pollution in Mexico City is another grave problem. Industry contributes 20 percent of the annual total of atmospheric contaminants to the MZMC: approximately 357,000 metric tons of sulfur dioxide, 118,000 metric tons of hydrocarbons, 104,000 metric tons of carbon monoxide, 83,000 metric tons of nitric oxide, and 348,000 metric tons of diverse particulate matter. Of the total number of industries located in the MZMC, only 30 percent have antipollution equipment, which in many cases is insufficient or inoperative.[14] Automotive vehicles are, however, the main polluters. In 1983, the state-run oil company, PEMEX, based on its own studies, classified motor vehicles as the principal source of pollution, producing 85 percent of the tonnage emitted daily.[15] The search for solutions is complicated by the explosive growth in the number of vehicles, the types of technology and fuels used in them, the lack of strict controls over the maintenance of motors, and the atmospheric conditions prevailing in the Mexico Valley.

Between 1940 and 1980, the number of automotive vehicles in the Federal District grew six times as fast as the population.[16] This predominance of private over public transportation and the higher fuel consumption of private vehicles has increased atmospheric pollution. About 33 percent of the total annual national fuel consumption—some three million cubic meters of gasoline and 400,000 cubic meters of diesel fuel—is attributed to vehicles in the MZMC. Yet, of the almost three million motor vehicles that operate, 97 percent are private cars used for only 19 percent of the trips per person per day. This private transportation consumes fifteen times more fuel per person transported than the mass transit system.[17]

Poor motor maintenance and the advanced age of the vehicles also contribute to pollution. Devaluation and inflation and the subsequent loss of buying power have increased the number of run-down vehicles on the road and impeded government efforts to replace older, polluting buses.[18]

The relationship between vehicle speed and air pollution contributes to the city's pollution dilemma. As the number of vehicles increases and average speeds decline on the Federal District's principal roadways, the situation becomes more grave. During peak hours (7–9 A.M., 2–4 P.M., and 6–9 P.M.), when 60 percent of the vehicles are in transit, the use of gasoline increases 1.5 times and exhaust emissions double the average.[19]

The geographic location of the MZMC further complicates the pollution problems of vehicles. Internal combustion engines produce more contaminants at Mexico City's altitude (2300 meters above sea level) than at lower elevations. Calculations indicate that altitude-induced inefficiencies mean the three million vehicles in the MZMC produce as much pollution as 6.3 million vehicles operating at sea level. A second disadvantage of the MZMC's location is its low wind velocity. The high surrounding mountains effectively reduce ventilation of the city's polluted atmosphere. This lack of wind turbulence combines with seasonal drops in temperature to produce thermal inversions that trap life-threatening levels of pollution in the city.

Photochemical smog is now a normal component of atmospheric pollution in the Mexican capital. High levels of sulfur dioxide have been detected in the MZMC, emitted principally by diesel traffic, electric power plants, and industry, even in apparently uncontaminated zones such as the south of the city, where it is blown by the wind.

In spite of the efforts of PEMEX to reduce contaminant particles in fuel, almost all private automotive transport continues to use gasoline with high tetraethyl lead compound content and only a minimal proportion of public transportation (1.2–1.5 percent) employs diesel fuel with low sulfur content. Leaded gasoline is a particular concern because of recent studies documenting high levels of lead in newborns.[20]

Recent steps by PEMEX to reduce lead in gasoline have had the paradoxical effect of raising ozone levels in the capital due to the absence of catalytic converters on most Mexican cars.[21] The Ministry of Urban Development and Ecology's relatively modest ozone standard of 0.11 ppm is exceeded on more than 300 days each year, more than twice as often as in Los Angeles.[22]

The Government Response

Developments in the last few years have placed increasing pressure on the federal government to take more direct and immediate action against environmental dangers, especially in Mexico City. A series of thermal inversions in the winters of 1985, 1986, and 1987 dramatically increased pollution levels in the metropolitan area.[23] The November 1984 catastrophic explosion of the PEMEX gas distribution facility at San Juan Ixhuatepec, a Mexico City suburb, which killed more than five hundred people, injured some five thousand, and forced the evacuation of one hundred thousand, also provoked public and media outcries for government action.[24]

Numerous government programs and agencies are attempting to address environmental problems in Mexico. At the federal level, the agency charged with prevention and control of atmospheric as well as soil and water pollution is the Ministry of Urban Development and Ecology, and, more specifically, the Subsecretariat of Ecology.[25] Within the federal government there is the Ecology Commission, which also has lower-level offices charged with responsibility for the state of Mexico. In addition, the Senate and Chamber of Deputies have several committees concerned with environmental problems, including a National Ecology Commission.

One significant response of the de la Madrid government to increasing public concern for the environment was the issuing of the so-called 21 Points in February 1986—a series of decrees that included reforestation projects, regulation of automotive pollution, relocation of especially

115

dangerous or toxic industries in residential areas, innovative pilot projects to use gas and energy sources more efficiently, water purification projects, and public education programs promoting environmental awareness. Significantly, the government promised (and delivered) a report on its progress in implementing each of these points eight months after they were issued.

The increasing gravity of the pollution situation in the capital and continuing public protests led to a new program of 100 Actions by the federal government. Announced in a January 13, 1987, meeting of the National Ecology Commission (created in 1986 and chaired by President de la Madrid), the "Program of 100 Necessary Ecological Actions" includes a number of emergency provisions for responding to grave pollution levels in the capital. These include forced closing of schools and of selected highly polluting industries during severe thermal inversions; compulsory inspection of motor vehicles; relocation of polluting and/or dangerous industries; prohibition of parking on important arteries in the city; and reforms of the laws regulating forests.

The 100 Actions were put into force during 1987 and 1988 and have a special focus on air pollution generated by automobiles and industry, both because of the gravity of the air quality situation in Mexico City and because of the visible nature of the pollution. They encourage relocation of schoolchildren and teachers and of industrial workers to avoid long commutes, prohibit the location of new factories in areas that already suffer high pollution levels and water shortages, and subsidize the installation of pollution control equipment in existing factories. Although the program has a particular focus on the metropolitan area, there are steps planned for a number of Mexico's most threatened rivers, reservoirs, and shorelines.

It is too early to judge the effectiveness of the 100 Actions. Skepticism among Mexican environmentalists runs high, however. Manuel Fernandez, president of the Mexican Conservationist Federation, has criticized the program as having "no timetable, no system of accountability, no enforcement mechanism." Others pointed out the lack of a specific budget for the program, estimated to cost $100 million.[26]

On March 1, 1988, a new General Law of Ecological Balance and Environmental Protection (Ley General del Equilibrio Ecológico y la Protección al Ambiente) replaced the earlier Federal Law of Environmental Protection (Ley Federal de Protección al Ambiente). Among the main features of the new law are the regulation of natural resource use as well as of pollution; the decentralization to state and municipal authorities of a wide range of policy development regulations and enforcement; a focus on the causes of pollution rather than just attending to its effects; and encouragement of the participation of nongovernmental actors in the environmental policy process.[27] Because of the new law's emphasis on enforcement and decentralization of important powers to local authorities, initial reactions to the new law by environmentalists have been positive.

Environmental Policymaking in Mexico

As recently as the mid-1970s, environmental problems in Mexico, as in much of the rest of the world, commanded only limited public attention. Under presidents Luis Echeverría (1970–1976) and José López Portillo (1976–82), concerns about environmental issues had a low priority. When the environment did reach the presidents' policy agendas, it came as the result of agitation by middle-level government planners, university researchers, and professional organizations, generally located in Mexico City. Even though it was included in the global planning documents favored by the López Portillo administration, "environmental policy as such was never mentioned in the president's major policy speeches, nor actively promoted as a major policy initiative at the national level."[28]

This changed with the beginning of Miguel de la Madrid's presidential campaign in 1982. De la Madrid pursued a three-pronged strategy to push up environmental issues on the agenda of Mexican politics: a program of popular mobilization, a strengthening of environmental statutes and better coordination of administrative responsibilities in the environmental area, and improved regulatory performance.

Perhaps spurred by the Institutional Revolutionary Party's (PRI) assessment of the likelihood of a Green party–like movement emerging in Mexico,[29] de la Madrid's government set up a series of impressive "consultative mechanisms" to arouse and channel awareness of environmental issues among the population. In a searching evaluation of environmental policymaking in Mexico, Stephen Mumme gave de la Madrid's administration the highest marks for its program of popular mobilizations. State and regional conferences brought together local political leaders from the PRI's sectors, government officials, scholars in the state universities, and citizen groups to discuss a new environmental program being proposed by the government and to identify environmental problems. These efforts appear to have succeeded in placing the issue of the environment permanently on Mexico's domestic political agenda and in uniting urban and rural, middle and lower classes in common cause.[30]

With his "consultative mechanisms" to arouse and channel popular concern for the environment, de la Madrid has made a clear contribution to focusing greater attention on the need for government action on the environment. But Mumme's assessment of two other areas—statutory reform and regulatory performance—is less sanguine. Despite SEDUE officials' protest that de la Madrid's measures are more than symbolic reform and represent a serious commitment to environmental improvement in the long run, Mumme concluded, "Unfortunately, the government's record fails to bear them out."[31] Mumme attributed this weak performance to both what he called "circumstantial problems" and "actual priorities." Mexico's economic crisis and the crushing burden of the foreign debt are among the principal "circumstantial problems" hindering the fulfillment of commitments to environmental programs.

"Actual priorities" refer, however, to aspects of environmental policymaking that are intrinsic to the nature of the Mexican political system. Mumme pointed out that rather than relying on sanctions and making the initial investments in costly abatement programs, the government opted for an approach to abatement that stresses moral suasion, planning, bargaining, education, data collection, and incentives. The activities of environmental interest groups are dealt with in the classic petitionary pattern of supplication and persuasion that often characterizes legitimate interest articulation in Mexico.[32]

It may seem at first glance that this is precisely the kind of strategy that Mexico should pursue under the prevailing conditions of extreme fiscal austerity. By relying on the traditional mechanisms employed by the state to encourage compliance by the private sector and interest groups, the government avoids difficult political confrontations and costly expenditures that would be necessary to strictly enforce regulations and punish violators. But as Mumme pointed out, this approach rests on the plans under way for conversion and decentralization of industrial activities that will require decades to take full effect. In response to increasingly grave environmental deterioration, the Mexican government appears to have retreated into more of a hortatory and less of an enforcement role with regard to pollution.

Moreover, the success of any decentralization strategy will require that new areas of industrial growth be under the same environmental restrictions to prevent pollution problems from merely being transferred elsewhere. Although the evidence so far is anecdotal, some observers of Mexican environmental policy are concerned that in some officials' desire to stimulate growth outside Mexico City they may loosen environmental standards in the new industrial growth areas. One senior US business executive was quoted as saying that government officials "don't care [about pollution] so long as a plant is going to be built away from

Mexico City and will create a lot of jobs."[33]

A hortatory approach to environmental enforcement may in the long run strain Mexico's limited financial resources more rather than less. The explosion of the PEMEX gas plant in November 1984 may ultimately cost the government dozens of times the entire 1983 environmental budget. Yet, according to Mumme, only this "planning by disaster" was sufficient to spur the government to begin to relocate hazardous industries outside the immediate metropolitan area.[34]

Clearly, Mexico cannot do everything at once. It cannot open its political system, dramatically restructure the economy, and spend unlimited sums of political and financial capital on environmental enforcement. Yet it is important to heed the judgments of experts such as Mumme that the Mexican government's record on environmental policy regulation has sought to defer high costs by responding to demands primarily through symbolic reform and by opting for low-cost, future-oriented solutions in the planning and development realm.[35]

The steps taken by the de la Madrid government are obviously welcome. Carlos Salinas de Gortari, the winner of the 1988 elections, is a brilliant and technically sophisticated leader who counts the former minister of SEDUE and current mayor of Mexico City among his closest personal advisers. The environmental law of March 1988 gives important new powers to the federal government and to local authorities, which, if exercised, could break with the hortatory tradition of Mexico's regulatory past. But any meaningful assessment of the status of the environment as a policy concern in Mexico in 1988 must also confront the fact that decades of neglect have brought the nation to the brink of environmental disaster in key sectors such as the urban problems of Mexico City or land use in the tropical areas of the southeast. The scale of these problems and the difficulties Mexico's authoritarian political system will have in addressing them caution against easy optimism that an environmental corner has been turned in Mexico.

Perhaps the most sobering aspect of Mexico's economic and environmental dilemma is that the strain on the country's urban services, the destruction of forests and rural habitat, and the pollution of crucial water resources are the unintended but nevertheless inevitable consequences of a style of development pursued by Mexico since World War II. This import-substitution model of development no longer serves Mexico as an engine of growth, and an alternative path of export promotion is being sought. But the model's heritage of overcentralized production, protected and polluting industries, and distortions between the rural and urban sectors will be the central concerns of Mexico's economic and environmental actions in the coming decades.

Powerful alliances of political and economic groups were forged in the creation of the import-substitution model. Those alliances are already being challenged in Mexico's search for a new model of economic development capable of overcoming the external financial constraints and excessive dependence on foreign capital and technology that ended Mexico's unprecedented growth since World War II. The journey to a new and less environmentally damaging pattern of development has barely begun. Tragically, this search comes at a time of economic travail—public sector spending is being slashed, wages cannot keep up with triple-digit inflation, and businesses are being driven into bankruptcy.

Any analysis of the problems Mexico faces and the approaches by the United States that are most likely to be effective in encouraging Mexico to take the hard decisions necessary to address them ends with a dilemma. The United States must proceed with the day-to-day business of the bilateral relationship with Mexico and utilize the mechanisms already in place as a result of border agreements on environmental cooperation to address environmental concerns between the two countries. By protecting its own environment, policing the export of hazardous substances and industrial processes to Mexico, and making available training and technical assistance, the United States will contribute to the solution of the current manifestations of the style of development pursued by Mexico.

The larger challenge the United States must face, however, is that these kinds of efforts will ultimately be inadequate to the task that Mexico must undertake. That task is no less than a fundamental restructuring of the prevailing development model and an acceptance by a majority of Mexicans of the political changes required to support such a restructuring. The emergence of strong challenges to the PRI from Cárdenas on the left and the National Action Party (PAN) on the right will force a public dialogue about the different directions that Mexico's future might take. Contrasting proposals on a range of issues from debt repayment to the agricultural sector will be offered by opposition parties whose combined votes (by official count) nearly equaled those of the PRI in the recent election.

If the United States is to be more than a mere bystander in this process of debate and change, it must develop both a far more sophisticated approach to Mexico than it now has and a greatly strengthened political will to ease Mexico's unbearable burden. The coincidence of new presidents in Mexico and the United States in 1988 and the inevitable policy reviews of the bilateral relationship that attend this simultaneous succession can offer just such an opportunity.

Notes

This chapter is based on a case study included in the World Resources Institute book, *In the U.S. Interest*, Janet Welsh Brown, ed. (Boulder, Colo.: Westview Press, 1990).

1. Mauricio de Maria y Campos, "Mexico's New Industrial Development Strategy," in Cathryn L. Thorup, ed., *The United States and Mexico, Face to Face with New Technology* (Washington, D.C.: Overseas Development Council, 1987), pp. 67–81.

2. Steven E. Sanderson, *The Transformation of Mexican Agriculture: International Structure in the Politics of Rural Change* (Princeton, N.J.: Princeton University Press, 1986), p. 40.

3. Mary Williams Walsh, "Sorgum Creates Joy and Trouble in Mexico as Corn is Supplanted," *Wall Street Journal*, July 31, 1985.

4. Ibid.

5. Gregg Jones, "Farm Crisis Forces Mexico to Enforce Sweeping Action," *The Washington Post*, August 30, 1989.

6. The MZMC includes the Federal District of Mexico City and the surrounding metropolitan area of the state of Mexico.

7. Instituto Nacional de Estadística, Geografía e Informática, Secretaria de Programación y Presupuesto (SPP), various documents, 1981–1986.

8. Personal communication with Jorge Legorreta.

9. Gobierno Federal, Programa de Desarrollo de la Zona Metropolitana de la Ciudad de Mexico y de la Región Centro, 1985, pp. 12–13.

10. Ibid., p. 12.

11. *Uno Mas Uno*, March 6, 1985.

12. Studies by Dr. Armando Baez of the Centro de Ciencias de la Atmósfera of the National Autonomous University and Professor Eduardo Rodriguez Mestre of the Autonomous Metropolitan University have identified various contaminants and heavy metals in the treated water of Mexico City. Because these materials combine with sulfuric acid also present in the wastewaters to form insoluble compounds, the metals do not present a danger to human health in the concentrations and forms in which they arrive in the fields. The microorganisms carried by the waters, however, are very dangerous for humans consuming irrigated crops. *Uno Mas Uno*, April 2, 1985.

13. Lester Brown et al., *State of the World 1987* (New York: W. Norton and Company, 1987), p. 52.

14. Comisión de Ecología del D.D.F., *Informe de Labores*, 1983.

15. Figures provided by the Cámara Nacional de Comercio (CANACO), *Punto*, November 12, 1984.

16. Statement by engineer Gerardo Cruickshank, spokesperson of the Comisión del Lago de Texcoco, *Uno Mas Uno*, January 13, 1985.

17. *La Jornada*, November 23, 1984.

18. Rachel Sternberg, "Mexico City: The Politics of Pollution," *In These Times* (October 7–13, 1987): 13.

19. *Programa de Desarrollo*, p. 51.

20. In a sample of 102 Mexican newborns conducted by Dr. Stephen Rothenberg, a former Harvard Medical School researcher, 50 percent of those born between March 1987 and the end of July 1988 had lead levels above 10.5 micrograms per deciliter (mcg/dl) of blood. Based on research in other countries, children with levels above 10 micrograms at birth tend to have slower rates of mental development. William Branigan, "Bracing for Pollution Disaster," *The Washington Post*, November 28, 1988.

21. Unfortunately, the high cost of the technology needed to produce unleaded gasoline means that it is less expensive for Mexico to buy imported unleaded gasoline than to produce its own.

22. Branigan, "Bracing for Pollution Disaster."

23. In the thermal inversion of January 1987, songbirds literally dropped from the trees because of pollution levels. In the inversions of 1989, visits of a few days by those unaccustomed to the pollution levels produced bleeding in nasal passages.

24. Jonathan Kandell, *La Capital, The Biography of Mexico City* (New York: Random House, 1988), p. 565. Sixty-six acres were razed by the explosions and fire.

25. The predecessors of this agency are: from 1972 to 1976, the Sub-secretariat of Environmental Improvement, a department of the Secretariat of Public Health and Assistance, and from 1977 to 1982, the Directorate of Ecology, a department of the Secretariat of Human Settlements and Public Works.

26. Sternberg, "Mexico City: The Politics of Pollution," pp. 12–13.

27. *General Law of Ecological Balance and Environmental Protection* (Mexico, 1988), Chapter II, Article 6.

28. Stephen Mumme, "The Evolution of Mexican Environmental Policy," paper presented to the XII International Congress of the Latin American Studies Association, Albuquerque, N.M., April 18–20, 1984, p. 17.

29. H. Jeffrey Leonard, "Confronting Industrial Pollution in Rapidly Industrializing Countries: Myths, Pitfalls, and Opportunities," *Ecology Law Quarterly*, Vol. 12, No. 4 (1985): 799.

30. Mumme, "Mexican Environmental Policy," pp. 18, 35.

31. Ibid., p. 26.

32. Ibid., pp. 29, 32.

33. Interview with Edward Wyegard, director of Arthur D. Little (Mexico), quoted in Leonard, "Confronting Industrial Pollution," p. 791.

34. Mumme, "Mexican Environmental Policy," p. 31.

35. Ibid., pp. 32–33.

16

Air Pollution and Urban Transportation

Robert Yuhnke

When traveling in Europe and/or Third World countries, one finds that the air quality problems that are the central focus of this session are not unique to Mexico City. We must recognize that Mexico City is one of the worst examples of a megacity, a phenomenon that is occurring around the world. We have seen, within this decade, that for the first time half of the human population is living in urban areas. This is a result of both migration from rural areas into cities and the massive population growth that has occurred around the world in this century. The total human population has increased from about two billion to five billion in this century, the last two billion of that occurring since World War II. We are beginning to see the accumulation of human populations in cities of the magnitude of Mexico City all around the world; cities like Shanghai, Peking, Tokyo, Los Angeles, New York, Cairo, New Delhi, and others demonstrate that this is a problem that must be addressed on a global scale. It raises a serious question as to whether or not it is possible to develop population centers of fifteen to twenty-five million people in one urban setting and preserve within that context breathable air, drinkable water, some presence of nature, and some sense of a relationship between human presence and a natural system.

The air pollution issue is one of the most demanding of attention because it affects all of us who live in these environments. Rich or poor, you cannot escape the air that you breathe if you live in these urban areas. That is a major factor in helping to develop the political support even now emerging in the Third World countries to begin to tackle these problems. But there is a serious question as to whether we can successfully strike the balance between preserving environmental quality and the quality of human life while allowing these urban centers of human settlement to occur. It is also important to recognize the cost of these kinds of pollution problems in human terms.

Robert Yuhnke is senior attorney for the Environmental Defense Fund.

Those of us who live in US cities, except for Los Angeles, really do not have a sense of the consequences of the levels of pollution found in Mexico City. In some cities I have had a difficult time breathing and have woken up gasping for breath. I have traveled with friends with lung problems who have been so seriously affected by pollution that they could not remain in those environments for more than forty-eight hours without feeling severe discomfort. Research has demonstrated a 15 percent reduction in lung capacity in teenagers who have grown up in Los Angeles—a significant reduction in the capacity of the human body to function—and an associated increase in lung diseases like emphysema. Ozone has been found in recent research to scar and cause permanent damage to the tissue of the lungs. Meanwhile we are creating urban settings where half of the world's population lives that are significantly affecting the ability of the population to experience normal healthy life. The severity of the effects of this pollution is beginning to stimulate action.

It is interesting to make some comparisons between Mexico City and Los Angeles. I choose Los Angeles because, as the most polluted city in the United States, it has a pollution condition more similar to Mexico City than any other in our country. It also has other dimensions of scale that make it comparable to Mexico City. Mexico City has nineteen and a half million people; Los Angeles, or at least what is called the South Coast Air District, has twelve and a half million people. Mexico City has two and a half to three million vehicles; Los Angeles has more than eleven million vehicles. Mexico City has approximately thirty thousand industrial emitters; Los Angeles has between eighteen and twenty thousand. Mexico City has two large electric power plants and Los Angeles has four. In terms of pollution concentrations, or the frequency of high polluting days, Mexico City is reported to have approximately three hundred violation days per year whereas Los Angeles averages one hundred and eighty. But the difference there is not so great when you compare Los Angeles with other US cities where the next highest, in terms of the number of pollution days, is Houston, with only forty.

Los Angeles is one of the richest urban environments in the world. It has a reasonably well-educated population living in a very healthy economic environment, which has been booming for the better part of two decades despite national economic trends that are occasionally negative. Los Angeles is a city in which you not only have severe pollution problems, but also the economic capacity and the political ability to tackle these problems in a way that Third World countries do not have. Los Angeles has implemented the most innovative technological approaches to urban air pollution in the world. It has really been the crucible for the development of pollution strategies. More pollution control technologies have been developed there for stationary sources for refineries, for example where nitrogen oxide controls are in use, than anywhere else in the world. The city has power plant controls far more advanced than any in use anywhere else in the United States and that are comparable to only a few controlled plants in Japan.

As a result of the magnitude of the problem in Los Angeles, the state of California has developed tailpipe emission control strategies that have pushed the limits of such technology to the degree that Congress, in looking at revisions to the Clean Air Act, is using the California tailpipe standards as the basis for new amendments that are likely to be enacted. These standards will bring the rest of the country up to the level of pollution control that the California Air Resources Board has developed for automobiles. As a result of these control strategies, cars produced today and sold in Los Angeles emit 90 to 98 percent less pollutants than they did in 1968. The dramatic reductions in per-vehicle emissions in Los Angeles has led to similar efforts in the rest of the United States to require significant control of tailpipe emissions. Those requirements have not been repeated outside the United States despite the fact that German, Japanese, French, Italian, and Brazilian motor vehicle manufacturers have to design and build cars for sale in the US market that can meet the California standards.

The European Community is just now beginning to move toward setting tailpipe emissions standards for Europe, largely in response to some of the serious urban air pollution problems there, as well as to the death of the forests. Korea, Taiwan, Japan, and Singapore are now beginning to move toward the adoption of tailpipe standards in Asia. The Chinese, however, are building their first automobile production plant and are not even thinking about instituting such controls, which is astounding considering the severe air pollution problems in China, which has relatively few automobiles.

Señor Menéndez's review of Mexico's move toward the adoption of tight tailpipe emissions controls is consistent with the pattern we are beginning to see around the world. It is important to recognize, however, that the tremendous advance in technology for controlling emissions from automobiles over the last twenty years has been spearheaded by demands for clean air in Los Angeles more than anywhere else. The pollution problem in Los Angeles has not been solved. It has improved, however, from the peak pollution levels of ten and fifteen years ago, when pollution alerts were announced and people were required to stay indoors, children were not allowed to go to school, and some industries were required to shut down temporarily. Those types of pollution alerts have largely been eliminated in Los Angeles, but still the peak concentrations are three times the national health standard and there are still 180 days each year, or one day out of every two, in Los Angeles when the air is not safe to breathe.

We have to recognize that the technological advances achieved in this country stem largely from having had the wealth to do so and also because it has been politically easier to lean on Detroit and demand cleaner cars than to pursue other strategies. It has not been enough to achieve the magnitude of emission reductions needed to clean up either Los Angeles or some thirty other cities in the United States where the pollution problems are not as severe but still have not been brought down to safe levels, cities like New York, Chicago, Denver, Houston, Atlanta, and Washington, DC.

We have begun to see the development of other strategies as well. One is to clean up the existing fuel. The majority of the vehicles that are now on the road burn either gasoline or diesel oil. California again has moved out in front, requiring new standards to remove sulfur from diesel fuels. California has also recently introduced a new standard to reduce air matter content. These measures combined will achieve an overall 35 percent reduction in the particulate emissions from diesel trucks and buses with no further steps required. It is a strategy that offers some dramatic potential for reduction.

ARCO recently announced that it is going to start producing a clean fuel for automobiles; clean, of course, is a relative term, but the new fuel blend is expected to achieve significant reductions in all the major pollutants: carbon monoxide, nitrogen oxides, ozone, and the carcinogens in tailpipe emissions, particularly benzene. These reductions, however, are not going to be enough to clean up cities like Los Angeles; other major initiatives will be needed.

Another set of strategies involves a complete shifting of fuels. New Zealand has taken the world lead in moving to natural gas as a vehicle fuel. They have already converted more than 150,000 vehicles, including standard family automobiles as well as buses and trucks, thus demonstrating what can be done on a large scale. They followed this strategy almost entirely for economic reasons, not pollution reasons, because they have a surplus of natural gas—the only domestic fuel available in New Zealand. Thus there was an incentive to move toward the use of a domestically available fuel rather than being dependent on the world fuel market.

Research being done in the United States today shows that compressed natural gas (CNG) may well offer one of the most significant across-the-board reductions in all of the major pollutants including carbon monoxide particulates and the ozone precursors. This has been initiated on a large scale in Texas where, again for economic reasons, the state legislature adopted two bills that will require all state vehicles to operate on CNG over the next four years; this will represent a shift of approximately thirty thousand vehicles. This kind of fuel shift, if it is done on a large enough scale to make a significant environmental difference, is going to require a major economic investment. Essentially we are talking about changing over the entire fuel infrastructure for a nation. Such a conversion will require installing large compressor units at each gas station to deliver compressed CNG to the vehicle fast enough so that people will be willing to accept it as a fuel. CNG tanks must also be put in all vehicles. The cost of converting a car in the United States is about $1,200–1,500 per vehicle, and the cost of installing CNG dispensing facilities at the average gas station is about $275,000. Conversion on a national scale or even a scale the size of Los Angeles or Mexico City will require a multibillion dollar investment. But this may be necessary investment if we are going to solve pollution problems.

The last set of strategies that we need to look at for cleaning up cities and trying to preserve their habitability has to do with reducing vehicle use. These strategies have been avoided in the United States largely for political reasons. The United States has a greater level of personal vehicle use than any other nation in the world. In Mexico City, private vehicles consume 93 percent of the fuel used in the transportation sector but provide only 19 percent of the trips. That percentage is typical of the world as a whole. In the United States, only 19 percent of the trips are in something other than the personal automobile, whereas in Europe, for example, 60–80 percent of all trips in most cities are in something other than the personal automobile. The United States has approximately 40 percent of the world's vehicles; at the end of the 1950s, we had 80 percent of them. The world is now rapidly catching up with us and the number of vehicles has grown to about half a billion in the world and is expected, by the end of the year 2000, to reach close to a billion.

Most of the increase in the vehicle population today is occurring outside the United States. The US population is saturated with vehicles. There are twelve and a half million people in Los Angeles and eleven million vehicles. The rest of the world, as its wealth increases, has begun to adopt the US "love affair" with the automobile. Vehicle populations are growing in some so-called Third World countries much faster than the human population as a relative ratio. The consequence of this is being seen in terms of the pollution effects.

In Los Angeles, even though we have achieved anywhere from a 90 to 98 percent reduction in per vehicle emissions of pollutants, the vehicle use patterns are increasing at such a high rate per year that we are offsetting the benefits of cleaner cars by increased vehicle use. In Los Angeles the increase in vehicle use per year is 3.5 percent, in Denver it is 4 percent, in Sacramento it is 5 percent, and in Phoenix it is 6 percent per year. These are Western cities with no history of significant public transportation. We have built cities around the automobile in the United States, which is part of the dilemma that we face when we try to tackle the pollution problem.

This is of significance, particularly from the standpoint that the reductions we have achieved for tailpipe emissions resulted from taking the older (pre-1981 particularly) dirty cars off the road and replacing them with much cleaner cars. In 1995, according to the EPA, the pre-1981 cars will be virtually gone from the highway. We will then all be driving the current technology of cleaner cars. This means that after 1995 we will no longer be getting an offset by replacing dirty cars with clean ones, and thereafter total emissions in metropolitan areas will be dominated by increasing vehicle use trends.

There is a lesson to be learned from Third World cities. Mexico City, with its three million vehicles—only approximately 25 percent of the number of vehicles in Los Angeles even though the population is half again greater—is meeting mobility needs of its population with a transportation system that in many ways is not planned. It has centered around formal public transportation in the form of buses and an informal jitney system that moves large numbers of people very efficiently around the metropolitan area. We are going to have to begin to look toward transportation alternatives to the automobile and find ways of moving people in less-polluting group travel. Otherwise vehicle use trends in the United States are going to overwhelm the pollution benefits that we have received from technological development. We have an opportunity to transfer the technological advances that we have made in fuel alternatives to Third World countries and also to learn from some of their patterns of efficient transportation a mechanism for adding transportation alternatives in the United States.

We have all become aware of the need to change the pattern of carbon dioxide emissions into the atmosphere. We have learned that the almost 50 percent increase in carbon dioxide concentrations in the atmosphere has already begun to stimulate a warming trend in global temperature readings. This, in turn, is resulting in increasing drought around the world, which, in 1988 for example, affected world food stocks significantly. It was the first year in anybody's record keeping that the United States grew less grain than it ate. This pattern was repeated in China, the Soviet Union, and Africa; even New Zealand had a dry year in 1988. This kind of pattern is not typical. We have seen a dramatic increase in forest burning in the United States that can be directly traced to higher temperatures. We are all familiar with the large amount of forest that was burned in Yellowstone, but what was lost in the press coverage was the fact that 1988 saw the largest amount of forests lost to fire in the entire history of the federal government's fire suppression program, which dates back to 1924. Two million hectares of forests were burned in 1988; in some cases that was related to drought and in other cases that was related to much higher temperatures. The forests are not capable of tolerating these conditions.

We understand the cause of global warming is carbon dioxide, and we know that in the United States emits 25 percent of the world's carbon dioxide. Thirty-one percent of that comes from transportation, and vehicle use in this country currently is increasing at a rate of 2.5 percent per year, which means that carbon burning from the transportation sector will increase by 40 percent between now and 2010. From a global warming standpoint we cannot tolerate this. As the rest of the world follows our lead in excessive vehicle use, this pattern will be followed in other countries, and global warming will be severely exacerbated. For that reason, we have to find alternatives to our pattern of vehicle use, and we are going to have to lead the way for Third World countries. We are going to have to find the alternatives and convince the rest of the world that they should not follow in our footsteps of the last forty-five years.

There is a set of issues here that links the patterns of urban development around the world. One of the most significant issues that faces all urban centers of significant scale is how to design an urban environment that will not demand that we use automobiles as the principal basis for transportation yet at the same time will meet the need for mobility in those environments. If we fail in that task, we will fail to achieve an environment for the human population that is acceptable from the standpoint of air pollution and we will also fail to address global warming. It is quite a task. The success of Mexico City in its efforts will be a real example of whether or not we can succeed in meeting this challenge.

17

Commentary

Rene Costales

Licenciado Menéndez has brought us up to date on not just the problems but also the emergency and medium-term measures that the Mexican government has implemented. Richard Nuccio discussed the congestion in some of the world's cities due to improper economic policies and the repercussions that they are having. This reinforces the fact that solutions to urban air pollution problems are related to the general macro-economic development models of the countries involved. He reminded us of Mexico City's water problem, which is intimately linked to its air pollution problem. We were also told that some of the measures necessary to improve air quality depend on the reforestation of the surrounding areas of the city, which will take a long time. Community organization may be one the keys to success in Mexico City in order to create the new ethic for reforesting the suburban areas. This is an important challenge.

I recently read a report on an economic study that measured what Los Angelenos were willing to pay per day to not be sick or not have headaches or trouble with their eyes. This was related to the amount of eye drops and cough medicines purchased, other medical expenditures, loss of employment opportunities, and loss of time at work. The study indicated that the benefits that could be derived from air pollution reduction were on the order of six or seven billion dollars. The Los Angeles case is interesting because the program that Menéndez described has a preliminary cost of approximately three billion dollars.

In any action program there are a multiplicity of measures that can be taken. For instance, about two years ago Mexican authorities decided to remove lead from gasoline. The result was insufficient octane in the gasoline and emission of unburned hydrocarbons in greater quantities. Through photosynthesis, this created the smog effect. The ozone levels then skyrocketed, so, in effect, a well-meaning measure taken on an

Rene Costales is a field officer in Panama for the Inter-American Development Bank.

emergency basis backfired. Now we are seeing a much more complete, more detailed, and more reasonable investment program.

One could probably say there has been underinvestment in air pollution monitoring and epidemiological studies. Epidemiological studies are significant because the scientific community itself still does not know, not even in the United States, what the real issues are in terms of which pollutant should be reduced first. In the United States much of the decisionmaking on pollution control is based on a few indicators, such as carbon monoxide, nitrous oxide, and sulfur dioxide. There are other carcinogens in the burning of fuels, like toluene and benzene, which, although in minute quantities in the air, are even more damaging. This underlines the need for investment in air pollution control projects, in the research, monitoring, and the analysis that will bring greater effectiveness over the years as the process of selecting and implementing control measures improves.

Note

Mr. Costales's comments are his own and do not necessarily reflect the opinions of the Inter-American Development Bank.

Discussion

The first question, directed to Robert Yuhnke, was devoted to the Bush administration's apparent reluctance to take the lead in international environmental protection. Elmer Cerin, an attorney, asked Yuhnke to comment on the Bush administration's position regarding alternate fuel legislation. The basic issue in Congress regarding alternate fuels, said Yuhnke, is whether to back the administration's proposal to mandate production of a minimum number of vehicles using alternate fuels (presumably methanol) or the alternative of setting standards for tailpipe emissions to drive the selection of fuel and technology combinations that would be most cost effective in achieving environmental objectives. Most environmentalists believe that we should not mandate a particular fuel until the environmental benefits of using that fuel are clear. Instead, they support allowing industry to develop technology capable of meeting government-imposed standards.

Major oil companies have a vested interest in opposing methanol conversion. ARCO is the only major oil company developing methanol blends. Conversely, most natural gas is owned by the oil companies, and they would prefer a shift to compressed natural gas, which could have greater environmental benefits than methanol. The drawback to CNG is the large initial infrastructure investment necessary to make such a shift; methanol uses existing delivery systems. Congress is very conservative, Yuhnke continued, and does not want to upset powerful interests by pushing the nation in a different direction. The Bush proposal calls for 500,000 alternate-fuel–burning vehicles by 1997, but no tailpipe standard is connected so there is no guarantee of any environmental benefit.

Edward Betzig, a retired foreign service officer, asked Yuhnke to explain US opposition to international conferences on environmental issues such as global warming. He remarked that Yuhnke's remarks suggested that the United States was pulling in the opposite direction from the rest of the world. Yuhnke responded that the administration position is not entirely clear. The appointment of William Reilly as EPA administrator suggested US leadership would be forthcoming, but signals from the White House suggest a diminished commitment. Reilly remains committed but lacks support within the administration. In January 1989, Secretary of State Baker discussed the possibility of the United States hosting a global warming conference and becoming a leader in the efforts to find a solution to the problem. The administration has backed off since then and has shown no interest in assuming a leadership role at conferences already scheduled for Europe. The strong statements on the environment from the Soviet Union and the United Kingdom make the US position even more troublesome, said Yuhnke. The United States is responsible for 25 percent of all carbon dioxide emissions and 37 percent of all CFC emissions. If we do not change our patterns of activity, we cannot expect others to do so. The Bush administration's actions suggest that the necessary leadership is not forthcoming.

David Mog of the Office of International Affairs at the National Research Council said he understood why Bush has resisted assuming leadership on global environmental issues. There would be enormous risks involved in committing our economy to unknown technology. He suggested that individual states might be able to assume leadership because they have smaller economies. Yuhnke responded that the most important strategy to pursue in a global warming context is energy conservation. In regard to shifting our economy, there is compelling evidence to suggest that the measures most likely to be used for energy conservation are cost effective regardless of their impact on global warming. California restructured the way that public utilities are permitted to earn income by shifting the emphasis from increasing capacity to improving conservation. The result is that there has been no increase in generating capacity or energy consumption in California in the past decade despite a population increase of 36 percent, from 22 million to 30 million.

The administration's reluctance to take a leading role is inexcusable, said Yuhnke, because improving conservation would not be disruptive to the economy nor reduce competitiveness. The Department of Transportation is developing a new national transportation program and Congress is evaluating transportation investment, the largest public infrastructure investment program in the world. The direction in which we spend our money will shape energy consumption in the transportation sector for the next twenty years. Thus, new legislation and policy will determine our contribution to global warming from the transportation sector.

The Environmental Defense Fund (EDF) has urged acceptance of the 1988 Toronto Conference on Global Warming recommendation of a 20 percent reduction in carbon dioxide emissions by the year 2005. The EDF has asked the Department of Transportation to incorporate this as an objective of the national transportation plan and to consider three strategies: a tightening of fuel emissions standards; an emphasis on fuel switching, perhaps to CNG for carbon reductions; and a shift in investment strategy from subsidizing automobile use to alternative public transportation such as subways. Los Angeles has recognized that they cannot allow an increase in vehicle use and achieve clean air. They have adopted a transportation plan designed to change vehicle use patterns with a goal of reducing the growing vehicle miles traveled by 60 percent by 2010. One obstacle, added Yuhnke, is that alternatives do not qualify for federal funding because federal spending is directed toward highway projects despite the virtue of the plan in environmental terms. It would not threaten national integrity to change our spending patterns, concluded Yuhnke, despite the administration's perception of a threat.

Jay Holmes of the US Department of Energy (retired) suggested that USAID and other US agencies lack the ability to look long range. He also noted that the Third World lacks the capability to conduct the monitoring and research necessary to answer the questions being asked. Rene Costales replied that Mexico does have the capacity to do some monitoring, but air pollution is the most difficult form of pollution to monitor. Costales believes that the scarcity of epidemiological research in the developing countries is even more significant. There are few clues as to the causes of death, and thus it is difficult to determine how to attribute these deaths to environmental factors. There are examples, however, of policy decisions made for health reasons. One of the best known is the removal of lead from gasoline. Although lead was initially removed so that catalytic converters could be installed to reduce air pollution, the complete removal was ultimately implemented due to health considerations.

The shortage of epidemiological research can have an impact on policy decisions, continued Costales. Brazil made a massive shift to ethanol, which reduced pollutants somewhat and reduced Brazil's dependence on foreign oil. No epidemiological studies have been conducted on the by-products of ethanol combustion and its impact on health. Clearly there are no short-term effects, but there is no evidence regarding potential long-term effects. Ethanol is expensive to produce; in fact it takes more energy to produce ethanol than is obtained through its combustion. Currently, gasoline-powered cars are seeing a resurgence in Brazil because ethanol is so costly. Additionally, Brazil is now importing ethanol. The shift to ethanol was implemented without sufficient epidemiological evidence regarding long-term effects and now also has proven to be an expensive alternative to gasoline. It should receive easy credit terms as a priority investment.

Richard Nuccio pointed out that the debtor countries have reduced public spending significantly. President Salinas recently told a joint session of Congress that when Mexico receives debt relief, it will spend a significant amount on environmental concerns. This was a clear statement of priorities and explanation of where funding will come from. Although the World Bank and the IMF are sensitive to environmental issues, future variations in the Baker and Brady plans need to be more sensitive to the need to increase public sector spending in selected areas, particularly the environmental sector. Even in the United States it is agreed that the state has a role in protecting the health of its citizens, which includes protecting the environment in which they live. The vast sums necessary for environmental protection must come from debt relief because the state will be responsible for funding environmental protection programs, Nuccio concluded.

Cross-border air pollution was of interest to another participant. Licenciado Menéndez was asked if petroleum companies will be allowed to relocate in Baja California to avoid US air emissions regulations. Would Mexico welcome this new investment or would environmental considerations take precedence, the speaker asked. She also reminded Menéndez that air pollutants blow north from Tijuana to San Diego. Menéndez reminded the session that he works for the government of Mexico City and not the federal government of Mexico. Furthermore, the prevailing winds blow south from San Diego during the day and north only at night, so Mexico is sending clean air to the United States. The brightest part of US-Mexican relations, he continued, is border pollution control. Mexico and the United States have concluded agreements concerning joint training and awareness programs for the maquiladoras on Mexican pollution legislation. These sessions are held in conjunction with the US Environmental Protection Agency. Additionally, equal emissions standards are found on both sides of the border. Although in the past companies may have been able to escape US regulations in Mexico, this will no longer be possible.

Index

About the Book

First in a series of short books designed to promote enhanced discussion and sharpened analysis of current public policy issues in Latin America, this collection of original pieces addresses the need to reconcile economic growth and environmental protection. The contributors—among them scholars, government officials, and development practitioners—provide a theoretical and practical discussion of sustainable development practices, explore alternatives to deforestation, consider the pros and cons of debt-for-nature swaps, and look at the enormous air pollution problems facing urban areas, especially Mexico City. The book presents new insights into the numerous problems—and potential solutions—confronting Latin America in the 1990s.